£600

GW00703440

THE
FIXED STARS AND CONSTELLATIONS
IN ASTROLOGY

THE FIXED STARS AND CONSTELLATIONS

IN

ASTROLOGY

by

VIVIAN E. ROBSON, B.Sc.

THE AQUARIAN PRESS
Wellingborough, Northamptonshire

First published 1923
This Edition 1969
Second Impression 1972
Third Impression 1973
Fourth Impression 1976

ISBN 0 85030 047 9 (UK)
ISBN 0 87728 033 9 (USA)

Printed in Great Britain by
Whitstable Litho Ltd., Whitstable, Kent

PREFACE

Of late years the subject of fixed stars and constellations has aroused the interest and curiosity of the astrological student who has been debarred from examining their effects owing to the lack of available information. Most modern textbooks of astrology are silent upon the subject except perhaps foi some tantalizing remarks upon the influence of the stars in cases of blindness, and for further details it has been necessary to consult a great number of old books that are difficult to obtain and in many cases prohibitive in price. For this reason there has been for several years an increasing demand for a book devoted solely to the astrological significance of stars and constellations, and the present work has been undertaken to meet this demand and to fill the most serious gap in astrological literature.

My object in compiling the mass of information here gathered together has been neither a critical nor an originative one. It has appeared to me to be desirable to place before the student as complete and systematized an account as possible of all that has ever been written about the stars from an astrological point of view, unburdened by alteration or criticism, in order that the work may stand as a foundation upon which future research may be built. For this reason I have obtruded few, if any, personal opinions or criticisms.

Originality is not claimed, but it is believed that the book will be found to contain practically everything that has been published on the subject since the Middle Ages, and to be as complete as it was possible to make it.   No pains have been spared to attain this end, and a free use has been made of all sources of information.   A detailed bibliography is unnecessary, especially as it would cover some two hundred books, but it is only fair to acknowledge my indebtedness to *The Science and Key of Life*, Vol. IV, by Alvidas, which contains much information on the effects of certain stars, and to R. H. Allen's *Star Names and their Meanings*, which I have followed throughout as the best available authority on the orthography and derivation of the names of stars.   The references throughout the text to Ptolemy, Wilson, Simmonite, Pearce and Bullinger refer, unless otherwise stated, to the *Tetrabiblos*, *Dictionary of Astrology*, *Arcana of Astral Philosophy*, *Textbook of Astrology*, and *Witness of the Stars*, respectively.   No plates or illustrations of constellations have been given for the reason that they would have added to the cost of the book without conferring any corresponding benefit.   The student who wishes to follow up the subject in a serious manner will, of course, require some kind of star map, or, what is much better, a celestial globe, but for the ordinary purposes of astrology not even a map is necessary.

If the present work has the effect of stimulating

the astrological study of the stars and encouraging research it will have achieved the purpose for which it was intended.

VIVIAN E. ROBSON.

CONTENTS

9

CHAPTER I

THE FIXED STARS IN ASTRONOMY

In the early days of astronomy the celestial bodies or stars were divided into two groups, the one consisting of the fixed stars and the other of the " erratic " or wandering stars which we now term planets. The fixed stars were thought to be immovable, and, although it was known that their positions with respect to the equinox were changing owing to precession, it was not until comparatively recently that the so-called " fixed " stars were found to possess independent motion and to be moving through space in immense and unknown orbits. It may, therefore, be remarked at the outset that to speak of " fixed " stars is really erroneous, but it will be convenient to retain the term here as there is an unfortunate tendency among certain astrologers to use the word " stars " in a would-be poetical manner for the planets.

Each fixed star that we see in the night sky is a *Sun* very similar to our own Sun in structure and general composition, and differing only in size and temperature. It shines by its own light and is probably surrounded by its own system of planets, though owing to the enormous distance no telescope constructed on present lines can ever hope to discover even the largest of such planets ; in fact were our Sun removed to the distance of the nearest of the fixed stars it would appear to us as a sixth magnitude star, and Jupiter, big as it is, would be totally beyond the powers of our telescopes. It follows from this that a great many of the visible stars and all the brilliant ones are immeasurably larger than our own Sun, which is a comparatively small member of the Universe.

DISTANCES. The distance of a star when expressed in miles is such an enormous quantity that the mind is unable to grasp it, and in order to reduce the figures to manageable dimensions such distances are usually expressed in *light years*, the unit of which is the distance travelled in one year by light moving at the rate of about 186,330 miles per second, namely, approximately six billion miles (6,000,000, 000,000). The distances of only a few of the nearer stars are known, that nearest to us being Bungula (α *Centauri*) at a distance of 4·3 light years, and one of the furthest Polaris at a distance of 44 light years.

The basic principle underlying the determination of the distance of a fixed star is simple and easily described. Suppose we measure the altitude of a star, or the angle between it and the horizon, on a certain night in the year, and again on a night six months later, when the earth is at the opposite point of its orbit. We know the diameter of the earth's orbit and we have determined the altitude of the star from each end of this diameter, so that we know one side and the two adjacent angles of a triangle from which the length of the other sides may easily be calculated. The difference in the angles so obtained is called the *parallax* of the star, and it is found to be only in the cases of the few near stars that any parallax can be measured, there being usually no appreciable difference in the star's position when viewed from opposite points in the earth's orbit.

MOTION. It has already been stated that the stars are by no means fixed, and there are in fact three distinct kinds of motion, viz. :—(*a*) Precession, (*b*) Proper Motion, and (*c*) Radial Motion, or motion to or from the earth.

(*a*) *Precession.* The precession of the equinoxes is a phenomenon that causes all the stars to appear to advance in longitude in a body at the rate of about 50″ per annum, due to the retrograde motion of the Vernal Equinox, or first point of Aries, through the constellations. The cause of this phenomenon is not absolutely certain. It is usually said to be due to a slight annual change in the inclination of the earth's axis, but it has been suggested that the effect comes from the motion of the Sun in space along its own orbit, by which, of course, all the planets would be carried along independently of their own paths just as the Moon is carried round the Sun by the earth. This precessional change does not affect the relative positions of the stars among themselves.

(*b*) *Proper Motion.* In the year 1718, Halley discovered that Arcturus and Sirius had moved southwards since the time of Ptolemy, and it is now recognised that all stars possess a proper motion of their own that causes them gradually to change their positions relative to each other. In all cases this proper motion appears very small owing to the great distances of the stars, though their actual velocity is no doubt exceedingly high. As seen from the earth the average proper motion of a first magnitude star is about 0″·25 per annum, while that of a sixth magnitude star is about 0″·04 but the actual rates vary in individual cases, the maximum proper motion known being that of an eighth magnitude star (G. C. Z., V, No. 243) invisible to the naked eye which is as much as 8″·7 per annum.

In common with the other stars our Sun is moving through space, and if, as we are sometimes told, this is the real cause of precession, it is probable that its orbit is one necessitating about 26,000 years for a complete circuit. The direction in which the Sun, and of course the whole Solar System, is moving at present is known, and the point which it is approaching, or the Apex of the Sun's Way as it is called, lies on the border of the constellation Hercules in R. A. 277° 5′ and Dec. 35° N, which corresponds to ♑ 11° and Lat. 58° N.

This universal motion of the stars has led to the suggestion that there may be a Central Sun round which the whole universe moves, and it has been suggested that Alcyone in the Pleiades is probably this body, but the suggestion does not find favour among present-day astronomers.

(c) *Radial Motion.* This is really only another form of proper motion that has recently been investigated. It is found that in the case of an ap-

proaching or receding body the lines in the spectro-
scope move and this has been used as a means of
measuring its velocity. The greatest velocity yet
found is that of μ Cassiopeiæ, which is approaching
the earth at the rate of 61 miles per second, while
other high velocities are ζ Herculis, 44 miles approaching; Aldebaran, 30·1 miles receding; and
γ Leonis, 24·1 miles approaching.

BINARY AND MULTIPLE STARS. Many stars that
appear single when viewed with the naked eye are
found under telescopic examination to be composed
of two or more stars lying very close together.
The simplest case of this is furnished by the so-
called *double stars*, in which the two stars are not
related in any way but appear close together because
of the angle at which we view them. Frequently
one is countless millions of miles further away from
the earth than the other, but as they both happen
to be nearly in line they appear to us to be close together. In the same way we may have triple and
quadruple stars accidentally grouped together. In
the case of *binary stars*, however, the two bodies are
actually related and revolve round each other,
while even more complex relationships may be
found in which three stars forming a ternary system
are all linked in the same way.

CLUSTERS. When a very great number of stars
appear together we have what is called a cluster, a
well-known example being furnished by the Pleiades.
The Milky Way also forms an enormous cluster extending right across the heavens. It is now thought
that the universe is disc-shaped, and that the Milky

Way represents the edge of the disc. If this is the case we ourselves and all our visible stars probably lie within it, for its thickness is estimated to be at least 10,000 to 20,000 light years, and probably much more. In looking at the Milky Way we are gazing along the disc from inside, and, therefore, an infinite number of stars appear to be crowded together, while looking at right angles the comparative scarcity of the stars is due to the fact that we are looking outwards from within the disc and the stars that we see form the top and bottom beyond which lies infinite empty space, unless as may well chance, other disc universes lie at distances so immense that their combined light fails to reach us.

NEBULÆ. Many clusters were known to the ancients, but as a rule they called them nebulous stars or nebulæ, as the components could not be separated with the inadequate means at their disposal. Nowadays, however, a great many real nebulæ are known. These consist of incandescent gaseous matter extending over many millions of miles of space and gradually condensing to form a star or solar system. They are in many stages of development, and their relative age can frequently be determined by their colour and spectroscopic composition. For astrological purposes nebulæ and clusters have always been grouped together, for at present we do not know what, if any, distinction should be made as to the nature of their influences.

COLOUR AND MAGNITUDE. Although it is not generally recognizable by the naked eye, the fixed stars exhibit a great variety of colour, and this, as will be seen later, was one of the early means of establishing the influence of a given star, though it could be applied only to the larger ones. For purposes of comparison the apparent sizes of the stars are denoted by numbers representing magnitude. The 1st magnitude stars comprise the brightest in the heavens, such as Sirius, Arcturus, and Aldebaran, and the remaining stars are classified in accordance with their apparent size and brightness down to the 14th and 15th magnitudes. Anything below the 6th magnitude is almost if not quite invisible to the naked eye and forms what is called a *telescopic* star. It is estimated that of the visible stars in the sky north of 35° S. declination there are 14 of the 1st magnitude ; 48 of the 2nd ; 152 of the 3rd ; 313 of the 4th ; 854 of the 5th ; and 2,010 of the 6th.

It is found, however, that certain stars appear to change in brightness and to vary periodically between certain magnitudes. Thus Algol varies between the magnitudes 2·3 and 3·5 during a total period of 2 d. 20 h. 48 m. 54·4 s., whilst the classic example Mira (o *Ceti*) varies between the 9th and 2nd magnitudes over a period of about 11 months. In the case of Algol the variability is caused by a dark companion star that produces a periodical eclipse as the two bodies revolve round one another, but the reason for the variability of stars in general is very imperfectly understood.

In addition to these periodic variables there are certain stars that show a gradual change of magnitude and others that blaze out temporarily and then diminish in light rapidly or disappear altogether. As an example of the former we have Zubeneschamali (β *Libræ*), which in the time of Eratosthenes was brighter than Antares (α *Scorpii*) and is now one magnitude fainter. The latter group covers the temporary stars or *Novæ* that suddenly appear from time to time. One of the most recent of these was Nova Cygni that was discovered by Mr. W. F. Denning, of Bristol, at 9.30 p.m., G.M.T., on 20th August, 1920, in R.A. 299°, Dec. 53½° N., corresponding to Long. ⋈ 1° 22′, Lat. 70° N. 50′, which was thought to have been connected with serious rioting and incendiarism at Belfast. The cause of the sudden increase in brilliancy of these bodies is not known with any degree of certainty, but it seems probable that in some cases it is due to the collision of two stars.

CLASSIFICATION. Several different methods have been used throughout the ages to classify and identify the stars, but almost all are based upon the fundamental grouping into constellations. In the days of Ptolemy only 48 constellations were recognized, the remainder having been added since 1600, but the origin of these ancient star groups is quite unknown. Forty-five of them were mentioned by Aratos in 270 B.C., but they were in existence hundreds of years before his time, and may have been formed by the Chaldeans or an earlier race of people. It seems certain, however, that the constellation figures were chosen for astrological reasons, since the arrangement of the stars in any group bears no resemblance to its traditional form. Originally only those stars falling on the constellation figure were recognised as belonging to the group, those outside being called " unformed " or " scattered," but at a later date the boundaries were extended and now every star in the heavens is a member of some constellation. Unfortunately the boundary lines are not by any means well defined, and may not be absolutely correct from an astrological point of view, for they have been settled only comparatively recently, Argelander's boundaries being accepted for the northern constellations, and Gould's for the southern. The original divisions were probably more regular, especially in the case of the zodiacal constellations, which are now of very unequal extent.

(*a*) *By name.* The earliest method of identifying stars was by name. All the large stars and many small ones bore distinctive names, most of which have come down to us. The Arabs gave nearly all the names in use in western astronomy, but they were probably outrivalled in their lists of star names by the Chinese, who seem to have had a very comprehensive system of stellar nomenclature. Identification by name has now been almost entirely superseded by other and better methods. At best it is a cumbersome system, which gives no proper clue to the approximate place where the star may be found, and moreover is hopelessly inadequate to deal with the countless small stars now revealed by the telescope. For astrological purposes, however, where only a comparatively few stars need to be considered, it is a much handier method than any other, and I have, therefore, retained the old names, and indeed added a few new ones where necessary, for it is much easier to talk of Sun conjunction Capulus, for example, than Sun conjunction 33 ♅ vi Persei.

(b) *By place in constellation.* Ptolemy made a certain advance in stellar identification by introducing the system of naming a star according to its position in the constellation figure, as, for example, " the Right Knee of Boötes " for Arcturus, but the system is a very cumbersome and inexact one, and of course fails completely in the case of stars lying outside the boundaries of the constellation figures. It was, however, in frequent use among the 17th century astrologers, and unfortunately has survived among those of the present day who pay attention to the fixed stars.

(c) *By constellation and letter.* In 1603 Bayer introduced a method in which each star was known by the name of the constellation containing it and further distinguished by a letter of the Greek alphabet. In assigning the letters it was usual to start with the brightest star, calling that α, and so on through the alphabet in order of brightness Thus Regulus, being the brightest star in Leo, became known as α Leonis, the genitive case being used for the constellation, and this system with slight modification is the one in use at the present day. It was, of course, necessary to introduce numbers as well as letters when the Greek alphabet became exhausted, and this was done by Flamsteed.

(d) *By catalogue number.* At the present time

it is usual to retain the last method for well-known stars but to identify the telescopic ones since discovered by their number in some reliable catalogue. Thus we have Groombridge 1646, Lalande 21285, and so on, these various catalogues containing the places of nearly a million stars, and giving the *mean* positions irrespective of precession, nutation, aberration, and proper motion. Thus almost every star can now be identified when once its Right Ascension and Declination are known, the use of longitude and latitude having long since been given up.

For the convenience of those who wish to investigate the influence of any star not dealt with in the following pages, the method of converting its Right Ascension and Declination into longitude and latitude is fully explained in the Appendix.

As Greek letters are extensively used throughout the text I append herewith the characters and names of the letters in the Greek alphabet:

α	Alpha	ν	Nu
β	Beta	ξ	Xi
γ	Gamma	ο	Omicron
δ	Delta	π	Pi
ε	Epsilon	ρ	Rho
ζ	Zeta	σ	Sigma
η	Eta	τ	Tau
θ	Theta	υ	Upsilon
ι	Iota	φ	Phi
κ	Kappa	χ	Chi
λ	Lambda	ψ	Psi
μ	Mu	ω	Omega.

CHAPTER II

THE constellations known to the ancients were but 48 in number, their names being as follows :

Zodiacal Constellations.

Aries	Leo	Sagittarius
Taurus	Virgo	Capricornus
Gemini	Libra	Aquarius
Cancer	Scorpio	Pisces

Northern Constellations.

Andromeda	Cygnus	Pegasus
Aquila	Delphinus	Perseus
Auriga	Draco	Sagitta
Boötes	Equuleus	Serpens
Cassiopeia	Hercules	Triangulum
Cepheus	Lyra	Ursa Major
Corona Borealis	Ophiuchus	Ursa Minor.

Southern Constellations.

Ara	Cetus	Hydra
Argo	Corona Australis	Lepus
Canis Major	Corvus	Lupus
Canis Minor	Crater	Orion
Centaurus	Eridanus	Piscis Australis.

To these many more have been added in comparatively recent times until their number is now well over 100. The original constellation figures are all traditional and have been a source of annoyance to modern astronomers, who have naturally failed to trace among the stars the slightest resemblance to the objects they are supposed to represent. To those actively engaged in a study of stellar and constellation influences, however, it will soon become apparent that these seemingly fanciful shapes are in reality a fair representation of the collective influences of the stars contained in them, and that the constellation of the Dog, for example, actually influences dogs, ridiculous as it may appear. This, of course, may be explained by assuming that the ancients based the figures and divisions upon their knowledge of the influence of each, but the same certainly cannot be said of the modern constellations and it is an amazing fact, though easily proved, that they also closely represent the nature of the influences.

The rationale of this is inexplicable and we can only suppose that the originators were in some way led to choose the most appropriate figure. That this has happened in the case of the planet Neptune is a fact well known to every astrologer, and it is none the less true that it is also apparent in the case of the constellations.

To those of an occult turn of mind the foregoing explanation will be adequate, but to the scientific investigator it will, of course, have no weight. If he will examine the facts in an unbiased manner, however, he will see that they are indeed facts, even if they appear at first sight to be unreasonable and absurd.

With this brief apology we may turn to a more practical consideration of the matter. The chief difficulty confronting the student is that each constellation occupies a fairly large part of the heavens and overlaps others when referred to the zodiac. Moreover the actual boundary line between any two constellations is not defined with any degree of certainty. It is probable that the chief effect of each is located in one or more particular places which are at present unknown. It seems, however, that the major points of influence lie in the vicinity of the important stars and also near the boundary of the constellation, which thus appears to play the same part as the cusp of a house. It must be remembered that a star may have its own effect apart from that of the constellation, which is the group influence of many stars, and therefore the two must be separated when endeavouring to fix the most sensitive points. It is also extremely likely that there may be sub-influences in each constellation, perhaps varying with the part of the figure on which a given group of stars may lie, and this is a matter that will certainly require attention in the future. In practice it will be found that the effect of the constellation is most marked when the Sun, Moon, or Ascendant is posited there. The conjunction, opposition and parallel have effect but the influence of aspects cannot be traced.

It will be noticed that Ptolemy expresses the nature of the constellations in terms of the planets, a method that will be found fully explained in Chap. IV. The other descriptions are modern and to be found chiefly among French authors. It will be observed that the characteristics of many of the groups resemble those of the sign in which they fall. Some years ago Sepharial suggested that the signs themselves might not be the real originators of all the influences ascribed to them, some of which might more properly be attributed to constellations. Thus in the case of Cancer the pushing nature of its natives may really be due to Monoceros, their love of dogs to Canis Major, and their love of the sea to Argo. This should be borne in mind for by careful research we may eventually be able to assign more exact influences to both signs and stars. In this connection it will be obvious that the separate influence of each degree of the zodiac may also be a stellar phenomenon.

A word is necessary, perhaps, as to the zodiacal constellations. These are actual irregular star groups lying along the ecliptic, or earth's path round the Sun, and should not be confused with the *signs* of the zodiac which are regular divisions of the ecliptic bearing the same names. In the descriptions given below comparatively little has been said as to the nature of these constellations because each has the same influence as the sign of the same name, and the latter are fully described in all textbooks of astrology.

In order to facilitate its use and avoid the necessity of consulting a globe or map the approximate extent of each constellation, both in longitude and declination, as nearly as can be estimated, is indicated against its name. In the descriptions that follow, the legendary history of the constellations has been given wherever possible so that students of symbology and occultism may exercise their powers of interpretation. In all cases, however, the Biblical parallels have been omitted, partly because they are often obvious but chiefly because they are later importations and not so worthy of study.

1. ANDROMEDA. The Chained Woman. ♈12— ♉15. 20N—55N.

Legend. Andromeda was the daughter of Cepheus, King of Æthiopia, and Cassiopeia. In consequence of Cassiopeia's boast that the beauty of Andromeda surpassed that of the Nereids, Neptune sent a sea-monster (CETUS) to lay waste to the country, and promised deliverance only on condition that Andromeda were offered as a sacrifice to it. She was accordingly chained to a rock, but was discovered and released by Perseus, who, riding through the air on Pegasus, slew the monster by turning it to stone with the Medusa's Head and claimed Andromeda as his bride.

Influence. According to Ptolemy the influence of this constellation is similar to that of Venus, though the legend would lead one to suppose some connection with Virgo. It is said to bestow purity of thought, virtue, honour and dignity upon its natives, but to cause battle with chimerical fears and a tendency to become easily discouraged. By the Kabalists it is associated with the Hebrew letter Pé and the

17th Tarot Trump "The Stars." If Mars af-flicts the luminaries from Andromeda, and especially if in an angle, it causes death by hanging, decapitation, crucifixion or impalement.

2. ANTINOÜS. ♑ 13—♒10. 8N—13S.

History. Antinoüs was a youth of extraordinary beauty, born in Bithynia, and was the favourite of the Emperor Hadrian. He is said to have drowned himself in the Nile in the belief that the Emperor's life would thereby be prolonged, and the constellation was formed in his honour by Hadrian in 132 A.D. Antinoüs has also been associated with Ganymedes who was seized by an eagle and carried off to be cup-bearer to Jupiter, but this legend belongs more probably to Aquarius.

Influence. No astrological influence was suggested for this constellation by the ancients, but it seems to have been associated with the ideas of passion, love and friendship, for certain of its components stars were named Alkhalimain or Al Halilain, the Two Friends, by the Arabs, and the Kabalists associated it with the Hebrew letter Vau and the 6th Tarot Trump "The Lovers." It has also been said to give a love of swimming, and to be connected with certain sex irregularities, the latter probably being greatest in that part of the constellation lying in Capricorn.

Note. Antinoüs lies just south of Altair in Aquila and is now taken as part of that constellation. He is sometimes represented as carrying a bow and arrow as he is borne aloft in the Eagle's talons.

3. ANTLIA PNEUMATICA. The Air Pump. ♍ 0—
　 ♎ 0.　30S—43S.

History. This constellation was added by La
Caille, 1752 A.D., under the name Machina
Pneumatica.

Influence. It is said to bestow prosperity, harmony and spiritual force.

4. APUS. The Bird of Paradise.　♐ 0— ♐ 25.
　 75S—80S.

History. This constellation was added by Bayer,
1604 A.D., under the name Apis Indica.

Influence. It is said to confer a kind, benevolent,
sympathetic and ambitious nature. This part of the
sky has apparently always been associated with birds,
for it was known to the Chinese under the names
" The Curious Sparrow " and " The Little Wonder
Bird." The connection of Gemini-Sagittarius with
flight may possibly be due to this constellation.

5. AQUARIUS. The Waterman. ♒ 9— ♓ 26. 5N—
　 30S.

Legend. Aquarius is said to represent Ganymedes,
son of Callirhoë, the most beautiful of mortals, who
was carried to heaven by an eagle to act as cup-
bearer to Jupiter. According to other accounts,
however, it is Deucalion, son of Prometheus, who was
translated to heaven in memory of the mighty deluge
from which only he and Pyrrha were saved.

Influence. Ptolemy makes the following observations : "The stars in the shoulders of Aquarius operate
like Saturn and Mercury ; those in the left hand and

in the face do the same : those in the thighs have an
influence more consonant with that of Mercury, and
in a less degree with that of Saturn : those in the
stream of water have power similar to that of Saturn,
and moderately to that of Jupiter." By the
Kabalists Aquarius is associated with the Hebrew
letter Nun and the 14th Tarot Trump " Temperance,"
over which virtue the constellation appears to have
some rule. The beauty of Ganymedes and his
flight through the air also link it to the ideas of
personal charm and aviation with which it is certainly connected.

6. AQUILA. The Eagle. ♑ 12—♒ 15.   22N—
13S.

Legend. Originally called Vultur Volans or the
Flying Grype, Aquila represents the Eagle, thought
to be Jupiter himself, that carried Ganymedes to
heaven (see AQUARIUS).

Influence. According to Ptolemy the influence of
Aquila is similar to that of Mars and Jupiter. It is
said to give great imagination, strong passions, in-
domitable will, a dominating character, influence
over others, clairvoyance, a keen penetrating mind
and ability for chemical research.   It has always
been associated with the sign Scorpio, and by the
Kabalists with the Hebrew letter Vau and the 6th
Tarot Trump " The Lovers."

7. ARA. The Altar. ♐ 10—♑ 0. 47S—65S.

Legend. During the war between the Gods and
Titans, the Gods leagued themselves together and

swore to withstand their enemies, confirming their oath upon an altar built for them by the Cyclops. After their victory the altar was taken up to heaven to commemorate the good resulting from unity. According to another account Ara was the altar on which the Centaur offered his sacrifices.

Influence. According to Ptolemy its influence is similar to that of Venus and also Mercury in some degree. It is said to give aptness in science, egoism, devotion and a love of ecclesiastical matters.

8 ARGO NAVIS. The Ship Argo. ♋10—♎20. 15S—65S.

Legend. This constellation represents the ship in which Jason brought the Golden Fleece from Colchis, said to be the first ship ever built.

Influence. According to Ptolemy the bright stars are like Saturn and Jupiter. Argo is said to give prosperity in trade and voyages, and strength of mind and spirit, but it has been observed to accompany cases of drowning, a notable instance being furnished by the horoscope of Shelley, where Argo occupied the 8th house and contained the Sun, Venus and Uranus. Drowning is particularly to be feared when Saturn afflicts the Moon in or from Argo. It is probably on account of this constellation that Virgo, especially the first decanate, is frequently found to be connected with drowning.

Argo was sub-divided by La Caille into Carina, The Keel; Malus, The Mast; Puppis, The Poop; and Vela, the Sails: but the separate influence, if any, of these divisions is not known.

9. ARIES. The Ram.   ♈18— ♉ 20. oN—27 N.

Legend. Aries represents the ram with the golden
fleece, a gift from Mercury, upon which Phrixus and
his sister Helle escaped through the air from their
step-mother Ino. On arriving in Colchis, Phrixus
sacrificed the ram to Jupiter and its fleece was hung
in the Grove of Mars, whence it was subsequently
carried away by Jason (*see* ARGO). According to
another account it was the ram that guided Bacchus
to a spring of water in the Libyan desert.

Influence.   Ptolemy's   observations   are   as
follows : " The stars in the head of Aries possess
an influence similar in its effects to that of Mars and
Saturn : those in the mouth act similarly to Mercury,
and in some degree to Saturn ; those in the hinder
foot, to Mars ; those in the tail, to Venus." By
the Kabalists Aries is associated with the Hebrew
letter Hé and the 5th Tarot Trump " The Pope."

**10. AURIGA. The Charioteer.   ♊10 - ♋3. 30N—
    60N.**

Legend. Auriga represents Erichthonius, son of
Vulcan and King of Athens, who was the first to
devise a chariot, drawn by four horses, which he
used in order to conceal his greatly deformed feet.
The goat and kids depicted in the constellation
figure commemorate the goat upon whose milk
Jupiter was reared, together with her offspring.

Influence. According to Ptolemy the bright stars
are like Mars and Mercury. The constellation is
said to give self-confidence, interest in social and
educational problems, and happiness, but danger of

great vicissitudes. The native is fond of country life and may be a teacher or have the upbringing of young people. By the Kabalists Auriga is associated with the Hebrew letter Samech and the 15th Tarot Trump " The Devil."

11. Boötes. The Herdsman. ♍ 27—♏ 7. 10N— 55N.

Legend. Boötes is said to be Arcas, whose mother Callisto was transformed into a bear (*see* Ursa Major) by Juno. While hunting, Arcas came upon his mother unawares in her form of a bear and pursued her into the temple of Jupiter, where he would have killed her and afterwards been killed himself by the priests. In order to prevent this, Jupiter, who had taken pity on them, took them both into heaven, where Boötes is still seen pursuing the Bear. According to another account Boötes is Icarius, who was killed by some shepherds he had made drunk with a flagon of wine given him by Bacchus. In consideration of the grief of his daughter Erigone and their hound Mæra, Jupiter placed her father in heaven as Boötes, together with herself as Virgo and the hound as Canis Minor.

Influence. According to Ptolemy the influence of the constellation is like that of Mercury and Saturn, though the star Arcturus is like Mars and Jupiter. It is said to give prosperity from work, strong desires, a tendency to excess, and fondness for rural pursuits, together with some liking for occultism. The Kabalists associate it with the Hebrew letter Teth and the 9th Tarot Trump " The Hermit."

12. CÆLUM. The Graving Tool. ♉ 12—♊ 15. 35S—50S.

History. Formed by La Caille, 1752, from stars between Columba and Eridanus. It is sometimes called Cæla Sculptoris, the Sculptor's Tools, and Scalptorium.

Influence. It has been said to give artistic taste and inclination, religious feeling, and fondness for astronomy, architecture and engraving.

13. CAMELOPARDALIS. The Giraffe. ♊ 2—♋ 15. 53N—90N.

History. This constellation was formed by Bart-schius in 1614 to represent the camel that brought Rebecca to Isaac.

Influence. It is said to confer patience, endurance, and great wisdom, and to cause its natives to become teachers or instructors of some kind.

14. CANCER. The Crab. ♋ 22—♌ 17. 2N—40N.

Legend. This constellation represents the crab that bit the heel of Hercules during his fight with the Lernean Hydra, and was placed amongst the stars in gratitude by Juno, the enemy of Hercules.

Influence. Ptolemy's observations are as follows : " The two stars in the eyes of Cancer are of the same influence as Mercury, and are also moderately like Mars. Those in the claws are like Saturn and Mercury." By the Kabalists Cancer is associated with the Hebrew letter Tzaddi and the 18th Tarot Trump " The Moon."

15. CANES VENATICI. The Hunting Dogs. ♍ 10—
♎ 5. 30N—50N.

History. Formed by Hevelius in 1690. They are represented by two greyhounds, the northern one named Asterion, and the southern Chara, held in leash by Boötes and assisting in his pursuit of the Bear.

Influence. This constellation gives a love of hunting and a penetrating mind, making those born under it faithful, keen, clever and fond of speculation

16. CANIS MAJOR. The Greater Dog. ♋ 0— ♌ 0
15S—40S.

Legend. This constellation is said to represent the dog set by Jupiter to guard Europa whom he had stolen and conveyed to Crete. According to other accounts, however, it was either Lælaps, the hound of Actæon ; that of Diana's nymph Procris ; that given by Aurora to Cephalus ; or finally one of the dogs of Orion.

Influence. Ptolemy states that the stars of this constellation, with the exception of Sirius, are like Venus. It is said to give good qualities, charity and a faithful heart, but violent and dangerous passions. There is some danger from, or fear of, darkness and the night, and liability to dog bites, though the latter characteristic is probably to be associated more particularly with Sirius. Canis Major is connected by the Kabalists with the Hebrew letter Tzaddi and the 18th Tarot Trump " The Moon."

17. CANIS MINOR. The Lesser Dog. ♋18—♋28. 1N—10N.

Legend. Canis Minor represents Mæra, the hound of Icarius, who drowned himself on account of his grief at the death of his master (*see* BOÖTES). According to another account it was Helen's dog who was lost in the Euripus.

Influence. Ptolemy gives no information as to the influence of the constellation itself, but merely desscribes that of its chief star, Procyon. By other authors, however, it is said to cause frivolity and either love of dogs or danger of dog-bites. It is noteworthy that the ideas of water and drowning seem to be universally associated with this constellation, for in addition to the Greek ideas embodied in the legends its Euphratean name was the Water-Dog, and its Chinese equivalent Nan Ho, the Southern River, certain of the stars being called Shwuy Wei, a Place of Water. Together with Canis Major this constellation is associated by the Kabalists with the Hebrew letter Tzaddi and the 18th Tarot Trump " The Moon."

18. CAPRICORNUS. The Goat.   25—♒22   10S— 35S.

Legend. During their war with the giants, the Gods were driven into Egypt and pursued by Typhon. In order to escape, each was forced to change his shape, and Pan, leaping into the Nile, turned the upper part of his body into a goat and the lower part into a fish, a shape considered by Jupiter worthy of commemoration in the heavens.

Influence. Ptolemy's observations are as follows
" The stars in the horns of Capricorn have efficacy
similar to that of Venus, and partly to that of Mars.
The stars in the mouth are like Saturn, and partly
like Venus : those in the feet and in the belly act
in the same manner as Mars and Mercury : those in
the tail are like Saturn and Jupiter." By the
Kabalists this constellation is associated with the
Hebrew letter Yod and the 10th Tarot Trump " The
Wheel of Fortune."

19. CASSIOPEIA. The Seated Woman. ♈25—
♊0   50N—70N.

Legend. Cassiopeia, the the wife of Cepheus and
mother of Andromeda, was taken into heaven in
consideration of the deeds of Perseus (*see* ANDRO-
MEDA). She is said to have boasted that not only
Andromeda but she herself was fairer than the
Nereids, and for that reason she was bound to her
chair and condemned to circle the pole head down-
wards as a lesson in humility.

Influence. According to Ptolemy this constellation is of the nature of Saturn and Venus. It is said
to give haughtiness, boastfulness and exaggerated
pride, but at the same time the power of commanding
respect It is associated by the Kabalists with the
Hebrew letter Beth and the 2nd Tarot Trump " The
High Priestess."

20. CENTAURUS. The Centaur   ♎2— ♏28.
28S—68S.

Legend. This constellation probably represents

Pholos, son of Silenus and Melia, who was accidentally wounded in the foot by one of Hercules' poisoned arrows. According to some accounts it is Chiron, but he is more correctly associated with Sagittarius.

Influence. According to Ptolemy the stars in the human part of the figure are of the nature of Venus and Mercury, and the bright stars in the horse's part of Venus and Jupiter. It is said to give hardheartedness, inclination to vengeance, love of arms, strong passions and an energetic nature. It may also be connected with poison.

21   CEPHEUS.   ♓ 17—♋ 0.   55N—85N.

Legend. Cepheus, King of Æthiopia, was taken into heaven with his wife Cassiopeia and daughter Andromeda in commemoration of the deeds of Perseus (*see* ANDROMEDA).

Influence. According to Ptolemy, Cepheus is like Saturn and Jupiter. It gives authority and a sober mind, sometimes making its natives judges or arbitrators, but exposes to cruel and severe trials. If Mars afflicts the luminaries from Cepheus, especially if in an angle, it causes death by hanging, decapitation, crucifixion or impalement. By the Kabalists this constellation is associated with the Hebrew letter Shin and the 22nd Tarot Trump " The Fool."

22.   CERBERUS.   ♐ 20—♑ 5.   16N—38N.

History and Legend. This constellation, which is not now recognized, was probably added by Hevelius in 1690. It represents the three-headed monster

that guarded the gates of Hades and was brought
to the upper world by Hercules. The figure depicts
it as held by Hercules, in which constellation it is
now merged. According to some accounts it is the
serpent slain by Hero that infested the country
around Tænarum.

Influence. Cerberus is said to cause faithfulness,
devotion, industry and watchfulness, and to restrain
from evil, but to give danger of poison.

23. CETUS. The Whale or Sea Monster. ♓ 17—
♉ 13. 10N—30S.

Legend. Cetus represents the sea monster sent
by Neptune to devour Andromeda (*see* ANDROMEDA).

Influence. According to Ptolemy this constellation is like Saturn. It is said to cause laziness and
idleness, but to confer an emotional and charitable
nature, with ability to command.

24. CHAMÆLEON. ♏ 12— ♐ 3. 75S—80S.

History. Added by Bayer in 1604.

Influence. Chamæleon is said to give a practical
and sound mind with a love of knowledge, a sympathetic and adaptable nature, and fondness for
travel and the drama.

25. CIRCINUS. The Compasses. ♏ 29— ♐ 10
55S—65S.

History. Formed by La Caille in 1752.

Influence. It is said to give a revengeful, violent,
grasping and tenacious nature.

26. COLUMBA NOÆ. Noah's Dove. ♊5—♋17
27S—43S.

History. First recognised by Royer in 1679,
but in existence some years before. It represents
the dove sent by Noah from the Ark.

Influence. Columba gives a gentle, kind, timid,
innocent and self-sacrificing nature, together with
strength of spirit.

27. COMA BERENICES. **Berenice's Hair.** ♍17—
♎12. 25N—31N.

History and Legend. Added by Eratosthenes in
A.D. 300. Berenice, the wife of Ptolemy Euergetes,
offered up her hair to Venus on condition that her
husband returned safe from the wars. The hair was
placed in the temple but was stolen, and to appease
the king's wrath it was said that Venus had taken
it into heaven to form a constellation.

Influence. It is said to give a suave and well-bred
manner, with great personal charm, but to lead to
an idle and dissipated life. There is some love of,
or ability for the stage. Lilly states that the
beginning of this constellation causes blindness or
defective eyesight, and it is probable that the part
lying in Virgo has some influence over baldness.

28. CORONA AUSTRALIS. The Southern Crown.
♑2—♑12 36S—45S.

Legend. This is said by some authors to represent a cast-off garland once worn by Sagittarius,
while others consider that it represents the wheel
upon which Ixion was tormented because of his

insult to Juno. This constellation has also been called Uraniscus, because of its resemblance to the palate or roof of the mouth.

Influence. According to Ptolemy the bright stars are like Saturn and Jupiter. It is said to bring unforeseen troubles, but to give a position of authority.

29. CORONA BOREALIS. The Northern Crown. ♏2—♏17. 27N—33N.

Legend. Corona Borealis represents the garland given by Venus to Ariadne on the occasion of her marriage to Bacchus after she had been forsaken by Theseus.

Influence. According to Ptolemy it is like Venus and Mercury. It is said to give artistic ability, love of flowers, lassitude and disillusionment, but to bring its natives to a position of command. By the Kabalists it is associated with the Hebrew letter Daleth and the 4th Tarot Trump "The Emperor."

30. CORVUS. The Crow. ♎5—♎15. 7S—25S.

Legend. Apollo gave a feast to Jupiter and requiring water sent the crow with a cup (CRATER) to fetch some On his way the crow noticed a fig tree, and, resting there until the figs became ripe, feasted himself upon them until, remembering his errand and fearing the anger of Apollo, he picked up a snake (HYDRA) and on his return gave as an excuse that it had prevented him from filling the cup. Apollo ordained in punishment that the crow should never drink so long as figs were not ripe, and placed the crow, cup and snake in the heavens as a memorial.

Influence. According to Ptolemy, Corvus is like Mars and Saturn It is said to give craftiness, greediness, ingenuity, patience, revengefulness, passion, selfishness, lying, aggressiveness, and material instincts, and sometimes causes its natives to become agitators.

31. CRATER. The Cup. ♍13—♎3. 5S—23S.

Legend. This constellation represents the cup given by Apollo to the crow (*see* CORVUS).

Influence. According to Ptolemy it is like Venus and in some degree like Mercury. It gives a kind, generous, cheerful, receptive, passionate and hospitable nature, with good mental abilities, but subject to apprehension and indecision. There is a disordered life full of sudden and unexpected events, and great danger of unhappiness, but usually some eminence.

32. CRUX. The Cross. ♏2—♏12. 56S—65S.

History. Usually atributed to Royer, 1679, but much older.

Influence. Crux is said to give perseverance, but many burdens, trials and responsibilities, together with much suffering and many hardships.

Note.—In connection with the rulership of countries it may be noted that Brazil was named the Land of the Holy Cross by the discoverer Cabral on 1st May, 1500, and that the constellation Crux has been represented on the postage stamps of that country.

c

33. CUSTOS MESSIUM. The Harvest-Keeper. ♉ 20—
  ♊ 10. 70N—77N.
History. Formed by La Lande in 1775 under the
title Le Messier, but not now recognised. It lies
near Cassiopeia and Cepheus.
Influence. It is said to give a simple, kind, retiring, pleasant and honest nature with interest in
rural pursuits.

34. CYGNUS. The Swan. ♑ 28— ♓ 28. 28N—
  55N.
Legend. In order to visit Leda, the wife of Tyn-
dareus, King of Sparta, with whom he was in love,
Jupiter turned himself into a swan and being pursued
by Venus in the shape of an eagle flew to Leda as if
for protection.
Influence. Cygnus gives a contemplative, dreamy,
cultured and adaptable nature. The affections are
ill-regulated and unsteady, and the talents develop
late. There is some love of water and swimming
and the arts. By the Kabalists it is associated with
the Hebrew letter Resh and the 20th Tarot Trump
" Judgment."

35. DELPHINUS. The Dolphin. ♒ 8—♒ 19. 3N—
  19N.
Legend. When Amphitrite, who was sought as a
wife by Neptune, hid herself, the God sent messengers
to find her. The dolphin was the first to succeed
and persuaded her to consent to the marriage, for
which service Neptune placed him in the heavens.
According to other accounts it is one of the pirates

who were changed into dolphins by Bacchus on his voyage to Ariadne.

Influence. According to Ptolemy, Delphinus is like Saturn and Mars. It gives a simple appearance, cheerfulness, dissembling and duplicity, love of hunting and sport in general but little happiness. There is fondness for pleasure, ecclesiastical matters and travel, but danger of suffering from ingratitude.

36. DORADO. The Goldfish.   ♈o—♊o.   48S— 67S.

History. Added by Bayer in 1604.

Influence. It gives penetration and a keen wit, fondness for appearances, artistic ability, but danger of obstacles and hindrances.

37. DRACO.   The Dragon.   Circles round pole. 63N—81N.

Legend. Draco represents the dragon that guarded the golden apples in the garden of the Hesperides. According to other accounts, however, it is either the dragon thrown by the giants at Minerva in their war with the Gods, or the serpent Python slain by Apollo after the deluge.

Influence. According to Ptolemy the bright stars are like Saturn and Mars. Draco gives an artistic and emotional but sombre nature, a penetrating and analytical mind, much travel and many friends but danger of robbery and of accidental poisoning. It was said by the Ancients that when a comet was here poison was scattered over the world. By the Kabalists it is associated with the Hebrew letter Mem and the 13th Tarot Trump " Death."

38. EQUULEUS. The Foal. ≈19—≈28. 0N—
12N.
Legend. According to various accounts Equuleus
represents Celeris, the brother of Pegasus ; or Cyl-
larus, the horse of Pollux.
Influence. It gives friendship and sagacity but
frivolity and love of pleasure.

39. EQUULEUS PICTORIS. The Painter's Easel.
♊0—♍5. 45S—65S.
History. Formed by La Caille in 1752 and usually
known by the name Pictor.
Influence. It gives imagination, artistic ability,
frankness and a reliable nature.

40. ERIDANUS. The River. ♓15—♊0. 0S—
55S.
Legend. Eridanus represents the river Padus or
Po into which Phæton fell when slain by Jupiter for
having set the world on fire by misguiding the chariot
of his father Phœbus.
Influence. According to Ptolemy all the stars
with the exception of Achernar are like Saturn.
Eridanus gives a love of knowledge and science, much
travel and many changes, a position of authority,
but danger of accidents, especially at sea, and of
drowning.

41. FELIS. The Cat. ♌28—♍15. 15S—25S
History. Formed by La Lande in 1805, but now
obsolete.
Influence. Felis is said to give a quiet, cautious,

watchful, careful, stealthy, cruel, revengeful and destructive nature, with fondness for out-of-the-way subjects and attached to home. The love of cats displayed by Virgo natives is probably due to this constellation.

42. FORNAX CHEMICA.   The Chemical Furnace.
Υ 10— $\text{\Huge 8}$ 13.   26S—40S.
History.   Formed by La Caille, 1752.
Influence.   Fornax is said to give an ardent, enthusiastic, persuasive, practical and pioneering nature with fondness for engineering, chemical or metal work.

43. FREDERICI HONORES.   The Honours of Fréderick.
Υ 2—Υ 20.   41N—52N.
History.   An obsolete constellation formed by Bode in 1787, in honour of Frederick II of Prussia, from stars between Cepheus, Andromeda, Cassiopeia and Cygnus.
Influence.   The constellation figure contains a nimbus to represent dignity, a laurel for fame, an olive branch for peace, and a sword and pen for war and literature. It is possible that some influence over these qualities may be inherent in the constellation.

44. GEMINI.   The Twins. $\mathfrak{S}$ 1—$\mathfrak{S}$ 23.   13N—35N.
Legend.   The constellation represents Castor and Pollux, the twin sons of Leda and Jupiter. It has also been suggested that it may represent Apollo and Hercules.

Influence. Ptolemy makes the following observations : " The stars in the feet of Gemini have an influence similar to that of Mercury, and moderately to that of Venus. The bright stars in the thighs are like Saturn." It is said to cause trouble and disgrace, sickness, loss of fortune, affliction and danger to the knees. By the Kabalists it is associated with the Hebrew letter Qoph and the 19th Tarot Trump " The Sun."

45. GLOBUS AEROSTATICUS. The Balloon. ≈9— ≈16. 26S—39S.

History. Formed by La Lande in 1798, but now obsolete.

Influence. It is said to give a dreamy, poetical, talkative, boastful, fickle and changeable nature. The sign Aquarius containing this constellation has always been associated with aeronautics probably on this account.

46. GRUS. The Crane. ≈7—)(0. 37S—56S.

History. Added by Bayer, 1604.

Influence. Grus gives a retiring, active, proud, watchful, kind, idealistic and devoted nature, with a liking for astronomy.

47. HERCULES. The Kneeling Man. ♎28—♑2. 5N—53N.

Legend. This constellation was put in heaven as a reminder of the labours of Hercules. According to another account, however, during the war between the Gods and Titans the former all ran to one side

of the heavens, which would have fallen had not
Atlas and Hercules supported it, and the latter was
placed in the sky in commemoration of this service.

Influence. According to Ptolemy it is like
Mercury. It is said to give strength of character,
tenacity and fixity of purpose, an ardent nature
and dangerous passions. By the Kabalists it is
associated with the Hebrew letter Daleth and the
4th Tarot Trump " The Emperor."

48. HOROLOGIUM OSCILLATORIUM. The Pendulum
  Clock.   ♓ 5— ♉ 14.   44S—67S.

History. Added by La Caille, 1752. It has also
been named Horoscope.

Influence. It is said to give a steady, patient and
industrious nature, a well-stored mind and a fondness for history.

49. HYDRA. The   Water-Snake.   ♌ 5— ♏ 23.
  10N—36S.

Legend. This constellation represents the snake
picked up and taken to Apollo by the crow (*see*
CORVUS).

Influence. According to Ptolemy the bright stars
are like Saturn and Venus. It is said to give an
emotional and passionate nature, threatened by
great troubles, and to cause some interest in shipping.

50. HYDRUS. The Snake.   ♑ 5—♓ 7.   62S—86S.

History. Added by Bayer, 1604.

Influence. It is said to give a cunning, practical
and treacherous nature, with great danger of
poisoning.

51. INDUS. The Indian.   ♑12—♒12. 45S—77S
History. Formed by Bayer, 1604.
Influence. It is said to give a quick penetrating mind, deep insight, and interest in orientalism, mysticism and sport.

52. LACERTA. The Lizard.   ♓18—♈5. 35N—50N.
History. Formed by Hevelius, 1690. The Sceptre and Hand of Justice, introduced by Royer in 1679, occupied the same place, but was superseded by Lacerta.
Influence. It gives a keen, practical intellect, a careful, patient and scientific nature, and a great love of power and justice.

53. LEO. The Lion.   ♌12—♍22. 0N—34N.
Legend. This constellation represents the Nemean Lion, originally from the Moon, that was slain by Hercules.
Influence. Ptolemy makes the following observations : " Of the stars in Leo, two in the head are like Saturn and partly like Mars. The three in the neck are like Saturn, and in some degree like Mercury. . . . Those in the loins . . . Saturn and Venus : those in the thighs resemble Venus, and, in some degree, Mercury." It is said that the stars in the neck, back and wing all bring trouble, disgrace and sickness affecting the part of the body ruled by the sign, especially if they happen to be in conjunction with the Moon. By the Kabalists, Leo is associated with the Hebrew letter Kaph and the 11th Tarot Trump " Strength."

54. LEO MINOR. The Lesser Lion. ♌ 10—♍ 7. 27N—45N.

History. Formed by Hevelius, 1690.

Influence. It gives a generous, noble, peaceable, but fearless nature, with the ability to undertake prominent and responsible positions.

55. LEPUS. The Hare. ♊ 5—♋ 3. 14S—25S.

Legend. A young man of the Isle of Leros greatly desired a hare and brought some over, for none were to be found on the island. The other inhabitants also wished to keep hares, but eventually the animals multiplied to such an extent that there was not enough food for them and they devoured the corn in the fields, whereupon the inhabitants joined together and destroyed them all.

Influence. According to Ptolemy, Lepus is like Saturn and Mercury. It gives a quick wit, timidity, circumspection, fecundity and defiance.

56. LIBRA. The Balance or Scales. ♏ 7—♏ 28 7S—24S.

History and Legend. Libra was not considered a separate constellation by the ancients and was called Chelæ, or the Claws of Scorpio, which sign was made to consist of 60°. The present constellation figure is said to represent the balance wherein Astræa weighed the deeds of men and presented them to Jupiter.

Influence. Ptolemy makes the following observations : " Those stars at the points of the claws of Scorpio operate like Jupiter and Mercury: those in the middle of the claws, like Saturn, and in some degree like Mars." By the Kabalists, Libra is associated with the Hebrew letter Heth and the 8th Tarot Trump " Justice.

57. LUPUS.   The Wolf.   ♏ 15— ♐ 7.   34S—57S.

Legend. The wolf is said to be placed in the heavens as a reminder of the religious nature of Chiron the Centaur, who is depicted as spearing it in order to offer it as a sacrifice.

Influence. According to Ptolemy the bright stars are like Saturn and partly like Mars.   Lupus is said to give an acquisitive, grasping, aggressive, prudent and treacherous nature, with a keen desire for knowledge, and strong ill-regulated passions.

58. LYNX.   The Lynx.   ♋ 0— ♌ 9.   36N—64N.

History. Added by Hevelius, 1690, and sometimes called Tigris, the Tiger.

Influence. It is said to give stealthiness **and** cunning, many changes in life, and an adventurous career.

59   LYRA   The Lyre.   ♑ 10— ♑ 29   28N—47N.

Legend. Mercury found the body of a tortoise cast up by the Nile, and discovered that by striking the sinews after the flesh was consumed a musical note was obtained.   He made a lyre of similar shape, having three strings, and gave it to Orpheus, the son of Calliope, who by its music enchanted the beasts, birds and rocks.   After Orpheus was slain by the Thracian women, Jupiter placed the lyre in heaven at the request of Apollo and the Muses. This constellation was often called Vultur Cadens, or the Falling Grype by the ancients.

Influence. According to Ptolemy Lyra is like Venus and Mercury. It is said to give an harmonious, poetical and developed nature, fond of music and apt in science and art, but inclined to theft. By the Kabalists it is associated with the Hebrew letter Daleth and the 4th Tarot Trump "The Emperor."

60. MACHINA ELECTRICA. The Electrical Machine.
$\math\{H\}$ 25—Υ 14.   28S—42S.

History. An obsolete constellation formed by Bode in 1800.

Influence. It is said to give a scientific spirit, a mind in advance of its time and peculiar or idealistic views.

61. MICROSCOPIUM. The Microscope. ≈0—≈6.
30S—47S.

History. Formed by La Caille, 1752.

Influence. It gives a careful, methodical, fastidious, meticulous and scientific nature.

62. MONOCEROS. The Unicorn. ♋0—♌16.
13N—23S.

History. Added by Bartschius, 1624.

Influence. It is said to give a pioneering, persistent, enterprising, ambitious and pushing nature, with a love of **travel and change.**

63. MONS MÆNALUS.   Mount Mænalus.   ♎12—
♎28.   10N—18N.
History.   Formed by Hevelius, 1690.
Influence.   It gives pride and dignity with great
abilities, but some destructiveness. The life is
beset by difficulties.

64. MONS MENSÆ.   The Table Mountain.   ♐10—
♒15.   72S—86S.
History.   Formed by La Caille, 1752, and now
generally known by the name Mensa.
Influence.   It gives an ambitious, aspiring and
proud nature. There will be many difficulties in
the life, but they will eventually be overcome and
the latter years will be peaceful.

65. MUSCA AUSTRALIS.   The   Southern   Fly
♏10—♏25.   66S—74S.
History.   Formed by Bayer, 1604.
Influence.   It gives a capricious, fickle, pleasure-
loving, changeable, but industrious nature.

66. MUSCA BOREALIS.   The Northern Fly.   ♉12—
♉20.   25N—33N.
History.   Added by Bartschius, 1624.
Influence.   It gives a practical, pleasure-loving
changeable and industrious nature, together with
sarcasm and spitefulness. There is a good deal of
vitality and favourable financial prospects.

67. NOCTUA.   The   Night   Owl.   ♏6—♏20
17S—30S

History. An obsolete constellation that superseded Solitarius, the Solitaire, or Turdus Solitarius,
the Solitary Thrush, formed by Le Monnier in 1776.
It occupies the end of the tail of Hydra.

Influence. It is said to give wisdom, discrimina-
tion, penetration, patience, and depth of thought and
study.

68. NORMA ET REGULA. The Level and Square.
♐ 2— ♐ 15.   36S—60S.

History. Added by La Caille, 1752. Sometimes
called Quadra Euclidis, Euclid's Square, but now
generally known as Norma.

Influence. It is said to give honesty, truthfulness,
justice and an upright life, with interest in Freemasonry, geometry, surveying, mathematics and
architecture.

69. NUBECULA MAJOR. The Greater Cloud. ♊4—
♋0.   65S—75S.

History. Probably added by Bayer, 1604.

Influence. It gives a poetical, artistic and imagi-
native nature but much hard work and powers of
persistence.

70 NUBECULA MINOR. The Lesser Cloud. ♈15—
♉4.   72S—77S.

History. Probably added by Bayer, 1604.

Influence. Similar to that of Nubecula Major but
gives isolation and loneliness.

71. OCTANS HADLEIANUS.   Hadley's Octant.
♐ 10—♒0.   75S—90S.

History. Formed by La Caille in 1752 in recognition of the octant invented in 1730 by John Hadley It is now usually abbreviated to Octans.

Influence. It is said to give a scientific mind marred by ill-regulated passions, psychic disturbances and discord.

72. OFFICINA TYPOGRAPHICA. The Printing Office
♋ 20— ♌ 10. 9S—22S.

History. Formed by Bode in 1800, but now obsolete.

Influence. It is said to give a keen and original mind, and honour through literature and art.

73. OPHIUCHUS OR SERPENTARIUS. The Serpent Bearer ♏ 27— ♐ 27. 18N—24S.

Legend. This constellation is said to represent the infant Hercules who strangled two serpents sent by Juno to kill him as he lay asleep in his cradle (*see* SERPENS).

Influence. According to Ptolemy it is like Saturn and moderately like Venus. It is said to give a passionate, blindly good-hearted, wasteful and easily seduced nature, together with little happiness, unseen dangers, enmity, strife and slander. Pliny said that it occasioned much mortality by poisoning. This constellation has also been called Æsculapius, and held to rule medicines. By the Kabalists it is associated with the Hebrew letter Oin and the 16th Tarot Trump " The Lightning-Struck Tower."

74. ORION. The Giant or Hunter. ♊6--♋2.
24N—13S.

Legend. The giant Orion was created out of an
ox-hide by the Gods, Jupiter, Neptune and Mercury,
at the request of Hyreus who had entertained them.
He was blinded by Œnopion and Bacchus for his
treatment of the former's daughter, but recovered
his sight by exposing his eyes to the rising sun.
In consequence of his boast that he could slay any
beast bred upon the earth the scorpion (SCORPIO)
was brought forth and Orion died from its
sting.

Influence. According to Ptolemy the bright stars
with the exception of Betelgeuze and Bellatrix are
like Jupiter and Saturn. It is said to give a strong
and dignified nature, self-confidence, inconstancy,
arrogance, violence, impiety, prosperity in trade and
particularly by voyages or abroad, but danger of
treachery and poison. It was thought by the
Romans to be very harmful to cattle and productive
of storms. By the Kabalists it is associated with
the Hebrew letter Aleph and the 1st Tarot Trump
" The Juggler."

75. PAVO. The Peacock. ♐25—♑25. 59S—77S

History and Legend. Formed by Bayer, 1604.
It is said to represent Argos, the builder of the ship
Argo, who was changed into a peacock by Juno when
Argo Navis was placed in the heavens.

Influence. Pavo is said to give vanity and love of
display, together with a long life and sometimes
fame.

76. PEGASUS. The Flying Horse. ♒27—♈10. 3N—36N.

Legend. Pegasus was born from the blood of Medusa after Perseus had cut off her head, and was afterwards tamed and ridden by Bellerophon. Being weary of earthly affairs Bellerophon attempted to fly to heaven but fell off, and Pegasus continued his course, entered heaven and took his place among the stars.

Influence. According to Ptolemy the bright stars are like Mars and Mercury. The constellation gives ambition, vanity, intuition, enthusiasm, caprice and bad judgment.

77. PERSEUS. The Champion. ♉12—♊8. 30N— 62N.

Legend. Perseus, the son of Jupiter and Danæ, was furnished with the sword, cap and wings of Mercury and the shield of Minerva. He killed the Medusa by cutting off her head and afterwards rescued and married Andromeda. On his return home he inadvertently killed his grandfather Acrisius and pined away through grief, whereupon Jupiter took pity on him and placed him among the stars.

Influence. According to Ptolemy, Perseus is like Jupiter and Saturn. It is said to give an intelligent, strong, bold and adventurous nature, but a tendency to lying. By the Kabalists it is associated with the Hebrew letter Lamed and the 12th Tarot Trump "The Hanged Man."

78. PHŒNIX. The Phoenix. ♒18—♈2. 42S—60S.

History.   Added by Bayer in 1604.

Influence.   It is said to give a pioneering disposition, ambition and power, together with a long life and lasting fame.

79.   PISCES.   The Fishes.   ♓ 15—♈ 26. 0N—32N.

Legend.   Venus and her son Cupid while sitting on the bank of the Euphrates suddenly saw Typhon, the enemy of the Gods, approaching them.   They leapt into the river and were saved from drowning by two fishes, who were afterwards placed in the heavens by Venus in gratitude for their help.

Influence.   Ptolemy makes the following observations :   " Those stars in Pisces which are in the head of the southern fish have the same influence as Mercury, and, in some degree, as Saturn : those in the body are like Jupiter and Mercury : those in the tail and in the southern line are like Saturn, and, moderately, like Mercury.   In the northern fish, those on its body and backbone resemble Jupiter, and also Venus in some degree : those in the northern line are like Saturn and Jupiter."   By the Kabalists Pisces is associated with the Hebrew letter Pe and the 17th Tarot Trump " The Stars."

80.   PISCIS AUSTRALIS.   The Southern Fish.   ♒ 15—♓ 5.   28S—36S

Legend.   This constellation is said to commemorate the transformation of Venus into the shape of a fish on one occasion when bathing.

Influence.   Ptolemy gives no separate influence

and only describes Fomalhaut, but according to Bayer the constellation is of the nature of Saturn. It is said to have an influence similar to that of Pisces, but, in addition, to augment the fortunes.

81. PISCIS VOLANS.   The Flying Fish.   ♍ 20—♐ 0.   63S—74S.

History. Added by Bayer, 1604. It is known as Volans.

Influence. It is said to give a quick mind, activity, emotion, imagination and poetical or artistic ability.

82. PSALTERIUM GEORGIANUM.   George's Harp.   ♉ 14—♉ 27.   o S—15S.

History. Formed by the Abbé Hell in 1781 in honour of George II of England, but now obsolete. It lies between the forefeet of Taurus and Eridanus. In the horoscope of George II the Sun and Venus were conjoined in Scorpio in opposition to this constellation.

Influence. It is said to give an harmonious and artistic nature together with joviality and kindness.

83. PYXIS NAUTICA.   The Mariner's Compass.   ♌ 19—♍ 3.   25S—36S.

History. Formed by La Caille in 1752 from stars in the mast of Argo.

Influence. It is said to give a wise, ambitious and steady nature, good judgment and interest in nautical and geographical matters.

84. QUADRANS MURALIS. The Mural Quadrant.
≏0—♏0   47N—57N.
History. Formed by La Lande in 1795 but now obsolete.
Influence. It is said to give a scientific mind, rectitude, justice, idealism and penetration.

85. RETICULUM RHOMBOIDALIS. The Rhomboidal Net. ♓8—♈22. 57S—70S.
History. Formed by Habrecht of Strassburg.
Influence. It gives a restricted life, self-absorption, tenacity, selfishness and emotion.

86. ROBUR CAROLINUM. Charles's Oak. ♍25—
≏12. 46S—54S.
History. Formed by Halley, 1679, in commemoration of the oak in which Charles II lay hidden on 3rd September, 1651.
Influence. It is said to give a frank, honourable, generous, hospitable and steady nature.

87. SAGITTA. The Arrow. ♐17—♒9. 15N—22N.
Legend. Sagitta represents the arrow with which Hercules slew the eagle that fed upon the liver of Prometheus.
Influence. According to Ptolemy this constellation is like Saturn and moderately like Venus, but Bayer states that it is of the nature of Mars and Venus. It is said to give a keen mind with ability for abstract thought and teaching or writing, irritability, jealousy and danger of hostility and bodily harm.

88. SAGITTARIUS.   The   Archer.   ♐ 28—♒︎1.
20S—50S.

Legend.   This constellation represents the wise
and just Centaur Chiron who was killed by accidentally dropping one of the poisoned arrows of Hercules
upon his foot.

Influence.   The following are Ptolemy's remarks :
" The stars at the point of the arrow in Sagit-
tarius have influence similar to that of Mars and the
Moon : those on the bow, and at the grasp of the
hand, act like Jupiter and Mars . . . those in the
waist and in the back resemble Jupiter, and also
Mercury moderately : those in the feet, Jupiter and
Saturn." . . . By the Kabalists Sagittarius is
associated with the Hebrew letter Vau and the 6th
Tarot Trump " The Lovers."

89. SCEPTRUM BRANDENBURGICUM.   The Branden-
burg Sceptre.   ♊︎0—♊︎4.   7S—31S.

History.   Added   by   Gottfried   Kirch,   1688.

Influence.   It is said to give honour, wealth,
eminence and power.

90. SCORPIO.   The Scorpion.   ♏︎23— ♐ 26 7S—
46S.

Legend.   This   constellation   represents   the
scorpion that killed Orion (*see* ORION).

Influence.   Ptolemy makes the following observations : " The bright stars in the front of the
body of Scorpio have an effect similar to that
produced by the influence of Mars, and partly to
that produced by Saturn : the three in the body

itself . . . are similar to Mars and moderately to
Jupiter : those in the joints of the tail are like
Saturn and partly like Venus : those in the sting,
like Mercury and Mars." By the Kabalists Scorpio
is associated with the Hebrew letter Oin and the
16th Tarot Trump " The Lightning-Struck Tower."

91. SCULPTOR.   The   Sculptor's   Workshop
    ♓ 4— ♓ 28. 30S—44S.
History. Formed by La Caille in 1752, its full
title being Apparatus Sculptoris.
Influence. It is said to give ambition, creative
imagination and artistic abilities.

92. SCUTUM SOBIESCIANUM.   Sobieski's Shield.
    ♑ 1— ♑ 11   5S—17S.
History. Formed by Hevelius in 1690 in honour
of John Sobieski III King of Poland.
Influence. It is said to give eminence, honour,
power, and bravery together with an adventurous
career.

93. SERPENS. The Serpent. ♏ 13— ♑ 15. 26N—
    17S.
Legend. When Glaucus, son of Minos, King of
Crete, was drowned in a barrel of red honey, Æsculapius was sent for to restore him to life and was shut
in a secret chamber with the body. While he stood
wondering what to do a serpent entered, which he
slew. Thereupon another serpent came in bearing
a herb which it placed on the head of the dead serpent,
thereby restoring it to life, and Æsculapius, using the

same herb, succeeded in restoring Glaucus. The serpent was placed in heaven and for this reason certain writers have identified Ophiuchus with Æsculapius. According to other accounts the serpent is one of those that would have slain Hercules in his cradle (*see* OPHIUCHUS).

Influence. According to Ptolemy, Serpens is like Saturn and Mars. It is said to give wisdom, craft, deceit, malice, a feeble will and danger of poison.

94. SEXTANS URANIÆ. The Sextant of Urania ♌ 22—♍ 10. 7N—8S.

History. Formed by Hevelius in 1690. He stated that he placed the sextant between Leo and Hydra because both constellations were of a fiery nature and formed a commemoration of the destruction of his instruments when his house in Dantzic was burnt in September, 1679.

Influence. It is said to give a keen, intellectual, orderly and exact mind with interest in mathematics, astronomy and similar subjects.

95. TARANDUS. The Reindeer. ♉ 23—♋ 0. 74N—90N.

History. Formed by Le Monnier in 1776.

Influence. It is said to give a quiet, gentle and retiring nature, and an obscure life.

96. TAURUS. The Bull. ♉ 17—♊ 23. 34N—2S.

Legend. Jupiter, assuming the form of a bull, mingled with the herd when Europa, with whom he was infatuated, and her maidens disported themselves on the sea-shore. Encouraged by the tameness of the bull Europa mounted it, whereupon the God rushed into the sea and bore her away to Crete. According to other accounts Taurus represents Io whom Jupiter turned into a cow in order to deceive Juno.

Influence. Ptolemy makes the following observations: "Those stars in Taurus which are in the abscission of the sign resemble in their temperament the influence of Venus, and in some degree that of Saturn . . . the stars in the head (except Aldebaran) resemble Saturn, and, partly, Mercury; and those at the top of the horns are like Mars." By the Kabalists Taurus is associated with the Hebrew letter Aleph and the 1st Tarot Trump "The Juggler." In all the ancient Zodiacs, Taurus is the beginning sign and marked the Vernal Equinox from about 4,000 to 1,700 B.C.

97. TAURUS PONIATOVII. Poniatowski's Bull. ♐ 24—♑ 17. 11N—5S.
History. Formed by the Abbé Poczobut of Wilna in honour of Stanislaus Poniatowski, King of Poland.
Influence. It is said to give obstinacy and changeability, emotion, honour and renown.

98. TELESCOPIUM. The Telescope. ♐ 24—♑ 15. 36S—59S.
History. Formed by La Caille, 1752.
Influence. It is said to give a keen mind, prophetic abilities, and interest in philosophical, occult or historical subjects.

99. TELESCOPIUM HERSCHELII.   Herschel's Tele-
    scope.   ♋5—♋16.   35N—47N.
History.   Formed by the Abbé Hell in 1781, in
honour of Sir William Herschel.
Influence.   It is said to give scientific abilities, **a**
keen intellect and spiritual powers

100. TRIANGULUM.   The Triangle.   ♉4—♉13
    30N—37N.
Legend.   Triangulum is said to have been placed
in the heavens by Jupiter at the request of Ceres who
asked that the shape of her island Sicily might be
represented amongst the stars.
Influence.   According to Ptolemy it is like Mercury.
It is said to give a just, companionable, truthful,
righteous and benevolent nature, with interest in
architecture and Freemasonry.

101. TRIANGULUM MINOR.   The Lesser Triangle.
    ♉6—♉12.   28N—33N.
History.   Formed by Hevelius, 1690.
Influence.   Similar to that of Triangulum.

102. TRIANGULUM AUSTRALE.   The Southern Tri-
    angle.   ♐5—♐22.   61S—71S.
History.   Attributed to Pieter Theodor of the
16th century.
Influence.   Similar to that of Triangulum.

103. TUCANA.   The Toucan.   ♒6—♒27.   60S—
    72 S.
History.   Added by Bayer in 1604.

Influence. It is said to give pride but gentleness unselfishness, activity and kindness.

104. URSA MAJOR.   The Greater Bear.   ♋10—♍27.   33N—73N.

Legend. Callisto, daughter of Lycaon, king of Arcadia, of whom Jupiter was enamoured, became a follower of Diana on account of her love of hunting. Jupiter sought Callisto by assuming the form of Diana, and Juno who discovered the intrigue turned Callisto into a bear. Angry that the bear was placed in heaven, Juno requested her brother Neptune never to let those stars set within his kingdom, and for this reason they are always above the horizon in Europe. To account for the length of the bear's tail, it is said that Jupiter, fearing her teeth, lifted her by the tail, which became stretched because of her weight and the distance from earth to heaven.

Influence. According to Ptolemy, Ursa Major is like Mars. It is said to give a quiet, prudent, suspicious, mistrustful, self-controlled, patient nature, but an uneasy spirit and great anger and revengefulness when roused. By the Kabalists it is associated with the Hebrew letter Zain and the 7th Tarot Trump " The Chariot."

105. URSA MINOR.   The Lesser Bear.   ♋0—♍7.   69N—90N.

Legend. According to some accounts this constellation represents Arcas, son of Callisto and Jupiter (*see* BOÖTES and URSA MAJOR). Other writers state that it is meant to represent Cynosura,

one of the Nymphs of Crete who reared the infant
Jupiter ; the other, Helice, being Ursa Major.

Influence. According to Ptolemy the bright stars
are like Saturn and in some degree like Venus. It
is said to give indifference and improvidence of
spirit, and to lead to many troubles. By the Kabalists it is associated with the Hebrew letter Tau and
the 21st Tarot Trump " The Universe."

106. Via Lactea. The Milky Way. Crosses ecliptic at ♊21—♋1.   ♐ 12— ♐ 20,   ♐ 29— ♑6
   Legend. Via Lactea is said to be caused by an
overflow of the milk upon which the infant Mercury
was nourished. According to other accounts, however, Saturn, wishing to devour his children, was
given a stone by his wife Ops and would have choked
had she not poured milk down his throat, some of
which overflowed and formed the Milky Way.

Influence. It is said to give a sympathetic, humane, artistic, kind and emotional nature. If the
Sun or Moon is afflicted here blindness is said frequently to ensue.

107. Virgo. The Virgin. ♍20—♏6. 16N—15S.
   Legend. This constellation is said to represent
Erigone, daughter of Icarius, who hanged herself
through grief at the death of her father (*see* Boötes).
According to other accounts it is Astræa, daughter
of one of the Titans, who sided with the Gods a-
gainst her own father.

Influence. Ptolemy makes the following observations: "The stars in the head of Virgo, and that at the

top of the southern wing, operate like Mercury and somewhat like Mars : the other bright stars in the same wing, and those about the girdle, resemble Mercury in their influence, and also Venus, moderately . . . those at the points of the feet and at the bottom of the garments are like Mercury, and also Mars, moderately." By the Kabalists it is associated with the Hebrew letter Gimel and the 3rd Tarot Trump " The Empress."

108. Vulpecula et Anser.   The Fox and the Goose. ♑ 24—♓ 4. 20N—30N.

History. Formed by Hevelius in 1690, and now usually abbreviated to Vulpecula.

Influence. It gives a cunning, voracious and fierce nature, together with a keen mind.

CHAPTER III

IN considering the classification of stars into groups, and the influences attaching to these divisions, it is necessary to include the lunar mansions, which are probably much older than either the constellations or the ordinary solar zodiac now in use. These mansions form a lunar zodiac of 28, or sometimes 27 divisions, each one of which roughly marks the distance travelled by the Moon in one day, and, although they undoubtedly underlay all the ancient systems of astrology, and three separate series have come down to us from Arabia, India and China respectively, all of which appear to be variants of some single lost system, our knowledge of their several influences is exceedingly meagre. More details are available of the Arabian system perhaps than of the others, and in this the influence of each mansion will be found to correspond more or less closely with the Ptolemaic nature of the stars included in it.

The method of employing the lunar mansions in practical astrology is not at all properly understood, and it is even doubtful how they should be measured. As given here they are in their original form and refer to groups of stars. Thus they are exactly analogous to the zodiac of constellations and may be used in the

68

same way as that is.   All the early series of mansions began with the star Alcyone, and presumably were fixed when that star marked the vernal equinox, but since then the starting point has been changed and in each case now lies in Aries, the 1st mansion being the 27th in the lists here given.   Used in this way they form a subsidiary series of constellations, each of which probably exercises a specific influence upon the bodies falling within its boundaries.

It is quite conformable to modern astrological practice, however, to refer the mansions to the ecliptic circle, making them each of equal extent, namely, 12° 51′, and beginning the 27th mansion in the lists from 0° ♈. In this way they would correspond to the zodiac of signs and retain their constellation influence sympathetically, just as the signs correspond in effect, though not in space, to the constellations. The former method is the original one and is still in use among Hindu astrologers, while the latter is utilized in the theory of the pre-natal epoch in which it is found that the initial degree of each mansion of 12° 51′ influences the determination of sex.   Furthermore it is known that many planets in these degrees bring fame or notoriety, the nature of which depends upon their sign and house position in the horoscope, and that the directional passage of the Moon from one mansion to another marks a change in the general current of events.   Beyond this, however, we have no information, and the whole matter needs careful investigation.   When referred to the ecliptic in this way, the initial degrees of the mansions are as follows :

♈	♋	♎	♑	0° 0′	12° 51′	25° 43′
♉	♌	♏	♒	8° 34′	21° 26′	
♊	♍	♐	♓	4° 17′	17° 9′	

In the following lists will be found the three main systems, namely the Arabic *manzils*, the Hindu *nakshatras*, and the Chinese *sieu* (Houses), with the longitude of the determinant star for 1st January, 1920, and as much information as possible as to the nature of each so as to form a basis for future study and research.

THE ARABIC MANSIONS

1. AL THURAYYA. *η Tauri.* ♉ 28° 52′.
The Many Little Ones. Profitable to sailors, huntsmen and alchemists. With Moon here in the case of an election, plant and sow but do not marry or travel by water.

2. AL DABARAN. *α Tauri.* ♊ 8° 40′.
The Follower. Causes the destruction and hindrances of buildings, fountains, wells, gold mines, the flight of creeping things, and begets discord. With Moon here, pursue business, travel, marry and take medicine.

3. AL HAK'AH λ with φ *Orionis* ♊ 22° 35′
A White Spot. Helps the return from a journey, the instruction of scholars, building, and gives health and goodwill. With Moon here, begin war but do not sow or undertake any good.

4. AL HAN'AH. γ *Geminorum.* ♋ 7° 59'.

A Brand or Mark. Favourable for hunting, besieging towns, and the revenge of princes, destroys
harvests and fruits, and hinders the operation of the
physician. With Moon here, plough, sow, but do not
travel.

5. AL DHIRA. α with β *Geminorum.* ♋ 19° 8'.

The Forearm. Favourable for gain and friendship
and for lovers, and destroys magistracies. With
Moon here, travel and take medicine.

6. AL NATHRAH. 44 M *Cancri.* ♌ 6° 7'.

The Gap or Crib. Causes love, friendship and
society of fellow travellers, drives away mice, afflicts captives and causes their imprisonment.
With Moon here, navigate.

7. AL TARF. λ *Leonis.* ♌ 16° 46'.

The Glance (of the Lion's Eye). Hinders harvest
and travellers and causes discord. With Moon here,
plant, build, marry, but do not travel.

8. AL JABHAH. α with γ, ζ, and η *Leonis.* ♌ 28°
   43'.

The Forehead. Strengthens buildings, promotes
love, benevolence, and help against enemies. With
Moon here, sow, plant, release prisoners but take no
purgatives.

9. AL ZUBRAH. δ with θ *Leonis.* ♍ 10° 12'.

The Mane. Good for voyages, gain by merchandise, redemption of captives. With Moon here, plant, marry but do not navigate.

10. AL SARFAH. β *Leonis.* ♍ 20° 30′.

The Changer (of the weather). Gives prosperity to harvest and plantations, hinders seamen, good for the bettering of servants, captives and companions. With Moon here, travel, navigate, sow, plough, marry and send messengers.

11. AL AWWA. β with η, γ, δ, and ε *Virginis.* ♍ 26° 2′.

The Barker. Gives benevolence, gain, voyages, harvests and freedom of captives. With Moon here, sow, plant, take medicine but do not travel or marry.

12. AL SIMAK. α *Virginis.* ♎ 22° 43′.

The Unarmed. Causes marital love, cures the sick, helps sailors but hinders journeys by land. With Moon here, dig but do not marry or travel.

13. AL GHAFR. ι with κ *Virginis.* ♏ 2° 40′.

The Covering. Favourable for extracting treasures, digging pits, helps divorce, discord, the destruction of houses and enemies, and hinders travellers. With Moon here, unfortunate for anything.

14. AL JUBANA. α with β *Libræ.* ♏ 13° 58′.

The Claws. Hinders journeys and marriage, harvest and merchandise, favourable for redemption of captives. With Moon here, buy cattle but do not navigate.

15. IKLIL AL JABHAH. β with δ and π *Scorpii.*
♐ 2° 4'.
The Crown of the Forehead. Improves misfortune, makes love durable, strengthens buildings and helps seamen. With Moon here, build, sow, plant, navigate but do not marry.

16. AL KALB. α *Scorpii.* ♐ 8° 39'.
The Heart. Causes discord, sedition, conspiracy against princes and rulers, and revenge from enemies, but frees captives and helps building. With Moon here, plant, sow, travel and go to war.

17. AL SHAULAH. λ with ν *Scorpii.* ♐ 23° 28'.
The Sting. Helps in besieging cities, taking towns, driving men from their places, destruction of seamen and captives. With Moon here, buy cattle, hunt but do not marry.

18. AL NA'AM. ζ with σ, τ, and φ *Sagittarii.*
♑ 12° 31'.
The Ostriches. Helps the taming of wild beasts, strengthening of prisons, destroys the wealth of societies and compels a man to come to a certain place. With Moon here, build, ask favours but do not marry.

19. AL BALDAH. π *Sagittarii.* ♑ 15° 8'.
The City or District. Favourable for harvest, gain, buildings, and travellers, but causes divorce. With Moon here, take medicine, navigate and put on new clothes.

20. AL SA'D AL DHABIH. α with β *Capricorni.* ≈2° 42'.

The Lucky One of the Slaughterers. Helps the escape of servants and captives and the curing of diseases. With Moon here, take medicine, travel, but do not lend money or marry.

21. AL SA'D AL BULA. μ with ν *Aquarii.* ≈11° 53'.

The Good Fortune of the Swallower. Causes divorces, liberty of captives and heals the sick. With Moon here, marry, sow, take medicine and lead an army.

22. AL SA'D AL SU'UD. β with ξ *Aquarii.* ≈22° 17'.

The Luckiest of the Lucky. Gives marital happiness, victory of soldiers but prevents the execution of government. With Moon here, build, marry, make friends and travel.

23. AL SA'D AL AHBIYAH. γ with α, ζ, η, and π *Aquarii.* ⨯ 5° 36'.

The Lucky Star of Hidden Things or Hiding Places. Favourable for besieging and revenge, destroys enemies, causes divorce, helps prisons and buildings, hastens messengers, hinders childbirth and hinders the action of the body. With Moon here, unfortunate for everything except taking medicine.

24. AL FARCH AL MUKDIM β with α *Pegasi.* ⨯ 28° 15'.

The Fore-spout (of the Water-bucket). Causes union, health of captives, and destroys buildings and prisons. With Moon here, plant, sow, bargain, marry but do not navigate.

25. AL FARGH AL THANI. γ with δ *Pegasi* and α *Andromedæ*. ♈ 8° 2′.
The Second, or Lower, Spout (of the Water-bucket). Increases harvests, revenues, gain, heals infirmities, hinders building, upholds prisons, causes danger to seamen and destruction of enemies. With Moon here, marry, take medicine, pursue business but do not travel or lend money.

26. AL BATN AL HUT. β *Andromedæ*. ♈ 29° 17′.
The Belly of the Fish. Increases harvest and merchandise, helps travellers through danger, strengthens prisons and causes marital happiness and loss of treasure. With Moon here, travel and take purgatives.

27. AL SHARATAIN. β with γ *Arietis*. ♉ 2° 51′.
The Two Signs. Causes discords and journeys. With Moon here, buy cattle, plant and take voyages. This mansion is now considered to begin the series.

28. AL BUTAIN. δ with ϵ *Arietis*. ♉ 27° 52′.
The Belly. Helps the finding of treasures and retaining of captives. With Moon here, buy and sell but avoid the sea.

Further details concerning the influence of the

Arabic mansions will be found in the chapters on Magic and Astro-meteorology.

THE HINDU MANSIONS

1. KRITTIKA. *η Tauri.* ♉ 28° 52'.
The General of the Celestial Armies. Symbol, a Flame or Razor. Regent, Agni, god of fire. Ruled by the Sun. A soft and sharp mansion or asterism belonging to the Brahmin caste and producing mixed effects. Those born on the lunar day will delight in white flowers, perform sacrifice, and will be magicians, metaphysicians, diggers, barbers, potters, priests or astronomers. With the Moon here at birth the native will be a glutton, adulterous, handsome and famous. Rules forests and the head.

2. ROHINI. *α Tauri.* ♊ 8° 40'.
A Red Deer. Symbol, a Temple or Wagon Regent, Prajapati, the creator. Ruled by the Moon. A stable asterism belonging to the Shudra caste and favourable for coronations, expiatory ceremonies, planting of trees, sowing of seeds, building of towns, and matters of a permanent nature when containing the Moon. Those born on the lunar day will be devout, rich, merchants, rulers, drivers, possessed of wealth and cattle. With Moon here at birth native will be truthful, polite, steady, handsome, cleanly and uncovetous. Rules vinegar pots and the forehead.

3. MRIGASIRAS. *λ Orionis.* ♊ 22° 35'.
The Head of the Stag. Regent, Soma, the Moon.

Ruled by Mars. A soft asterism belonging to the serving caste and favourable for friendship, married love, purchase and making of clothes and ornaments, music, and auspicious deeds when containing the Moon. Those born on the lunar day will deal in perfumes, flowers, ornaments, and animals, will be lascivious and good writers or painters. With Moon here at birth native will be timid, capricious, skilful, talkative, rich, fond of pleasure. Rules cots and the brows.

4. ARDRA. α *Orionis*. ♊ 27° 38′.

Moist, so called because of its stormy influence. Symbol, a Gem. Regent, Rudra, the storm god. Ruled by the Dragon's Head. A sharp asterism belonging to the butcher caste and favourable for punishment, torture, imprisonment, exorcism. mesmerism and separation or union when containing the Moon. Those born on the lunar day will deal in pod-grains, black magic, sorcery, exorcism, and will delight in murder, torture, lying, theft, cheating and adultery. With Moon here at birth native will be insincere, proud, ungrateful, cruel, sinful, deceitful and wicked. Rules temples and the eyes.

5. PUNARVARSU. β *Geminorum*. ♋ 22° 7′.

The Two Good Again. Regent, Aditi, the sky goddess. Ruled by Jupiter. An asterism belonging to the Vaisya caste and favourable for shaving Those born on the lunar day will be truthful, generous, cleanly, respectable, handsome, famous and wealthy, fond of service, friendly with painters and sculptors, honourable merchants. With Moon here at birth native will be devout, quiet, happy, good-tempered, of wrong views, sickly, thirsty and pleased with trifles. Rules granaries and the nose.

6. PUSHYA. δ *Cancri*. ♌ 7° 36'.

A Flower. Symbol, a Crescent on the Head of an Arrow. Regent, Brihaspati, the teacher of the gods. Ruled by Saturn. A light asterism belonging to the Kshattriya caste and favourable for sales, art, sculpture, learning, marital love, wearing of ornaments, medicine and purchase of carriages when containing the moon. Those born on the lunar day will deal in barley, cereals, crops, will be ministers or rulers and will live by water. With Moon here at birth, native will be popular, self-controlled, learned, wealthy, and charitable. Rules houses and the face or upper lip.

7. ASLESHA. ε *Hydræ*. ♌ 11° 14'.

The Embracer. Symbol, a Wheel. Regents, Sarpas, the Serpents. Ruled by Mercury. A sharp asterism belonging to the lowest caste and favourable for punishment, torture, imprisonment, exorcism, mesmerism and separation or union when containing the Moon. Those born on the lunar day will deal in perfumes, roots, fruits, reptiles and poison, will be skilled in medicine and dishonest. With Moon here at birth native will be dishonest, ungrateful, a clever swindler and a promiscuous eater. Rules dust heaps and the ears or lower lip.

8. MAGHA. *a Leonis.* ♌ 28° 43′.

The Mighty. Symbol, a House. Regents, the Pitris, Fathers. Ruled by the Dragon's Tail. A severe asterism belonging to the Shudra caste and favourable for acts of disgrace, destruction, deceit, imprisonment, beating, burning and poison when containing the Moon. Those born on the lunar day will be wealthy, fond of hills, merchants, valiant, and women haters. With Moon here at birth native will be wealthy, religious, contented, well served, and fond of life. Rules grain boxes and the lips and upper mouth.

9. PURVA PHALGUNI. *δ Leonis.* ♍ · 10° 12′.

The Former Bad One. Symbol, a Bed or Couch. Regents, the Adityas, Aryaman and Bagha. Ruled by Venus. A severe asterism belonging to the Brahmin caste and favourable for acts of disgrace, destruction, deceit, imprisonment, beating, burning and poison when containing the Moon. Those born on the lunar day will be fond of women, dancing, art and trade, will remain youthful and deal in natural produce. With Moon here at birth native will be generous, handsome, submissive, of wandering habits and good speech. Rules uninhabited houses and the right arm.

10. UTTARA PHALGUNI. *β Leonis* ♍ 20° 30′.

The Latter Bad One. Symbol, a Bed or Couch. Regents, the Adityas, Aryaman and Bagha. Ruled by the Sun. A stable asterism belonging to the Kshattriya caste and favourable for coronations, expiatory ceremonies, planting of trees, sowing of seeds, building of towns, and matters of a permanent nature when containing the Moon. Those born on the lunar day will be mild, cleanly, wealthy, virtuous, generous, learned, modest and heretical and will have influential friends. With Moon here at birth native will be popular, learned, free from cares and will have an enjoyable life. Rules lakes and the left arm.

11   HASTA. δ *Corvi.* $\simeq$ 12° 20′.

The Hand. Regent, Savitar, the Sun. Ruled by the Moon. A light asterism belonging to the Vaisya caste and favourable for sales, art, sculpture, learning, marital love, wearing of ornaments, medicine, and purchase of carriages when containing the Moon. Those born on the lunar day will be thieves, dealers in large animals, painters, merchants, handsome and religious. With Moon here at birth native will be active, resourceful, shameless, merciless, and a thief and drunkard. Rules tanks and the fingers.

12.   CITRA.   *a Virginis.* $\simeq$ 22° 43′.

Bright. Symbol, a Lamp or Pearl. Regent, Tvashtar, the artificer. Ruled by Mars. A soft asterism belonging to the serving caste and favourable for friendship, married love, purchase and making clothes and ornaments, music and auspicious deeds when containing the Moon. Those born on the lunar day will be mathematicians, surgeons, oculists, weavers, writers, singers, manufacturers of perfumes and dealers in jewels and cloth. With

Moon here at birth native will be fond of clothes
and flowers of many colours and will have beautiful
eyes and limbs. Rules water banks and the neck.

13. SVATI. *a Boötis.* ♎ 23° 7′

The Good Goer, or Sword. Also called Nishtya,
Outcast. Symbol, a Coral Bead, Gem, or Pearl.
Regent, Vayu, the god of the wind. Ruled by the
Dragon's Head. A mutable asterism belonging to
the butcher caste and favourable for commencing
work of an impermanent or moving character.
Those born on the lunar day will be weak, abste-
mious, skilful, fond of animals and changeable in
friendship. With Moon here at birth native will be
quiet, polite, self-controlled, skilful, kind-hearted
and charitable. Rules rice fields and the breast.

14. VISAKHA. *a Libræ.* ♏ 13° 58′.

Branched. Symbol, a Decorated Gateway. Regent, Indragni. Ruled by Jupiter. A soft and sharp
asterism belonging to the lowest caste and producing
mixed effects. Those born on the lunar day will be
religious, dealers in produce, and fond of red flowers.
With Moon here at birth native will be jealous, mean,
miserly, good-looking, clever in speech, and quarrelsome. Rules cotton fields and the nipples.

15. ANURADHA. *δ Scorpii.* ♐ 1° 27′.

Propitious or Successful. Symbol, a Row or
Ridge. Regent, Mitra, one of the Adityas. Ruled
by Saturn. A soft asterism belonging to the Shudra
caste and favourable for friendship, married love,

purchase and making of clothes and ornaments, music and auspicious deeds when containing the Moon. Those born on the lunar day will be valiant, influential and keep vehicles. With Moon here at birth native will be wealthy, of wandering habits, unable to bear hunger and resident abroad. Rules fields overgrown with flowers, and the stomach.

16. JYESTHA. α *Scorpii*. ♐ 8° 39′.
Oldest. Symbol, a Pendent Ear Jewel. Regent, Indra, the sky goddess. Ruled by Mercury. A sharp asterism belonging to the serving caste and favourable for punishment, torture, imprisonment, exorcism, mesmerism and separation or union when containing the Moon. Those born on the lunar day will be valiant, wealthy, famous, well born, somewhat dishonest, fond of travelling and in a high position. With Moon here at birth native will be cheerful, irascible, charitable, but will have few friends. Rules deserts and the right side of the body.

17. MULA. λ *Scorpii*. ♐ 23° 28′.
The Root. Symbol, a Lion's Tail. Regent Nirrity, Calamity. Also called Vicritau, the Two Releasers, as the stars in this mansion were thought to bring relief from lingering diseases. Ruled by the Dragon's Tail. A sharp asterism belonging to the butcher caste and favourable for punishment, torture, imprisonment, exorcism, mesmerism and separation or union when containing the Moon.

Those born on the lunar day will be druggists, dealers in flowers and fruit, rich and fond of gardening. With Moon here at birth native will be conceited, wealthy, luxurious, kind-hearted, happy and resolute. Rules stables and the left side of the body.

18. PURVA ASHADHA. ζ *Sagittarii.* ♐ 12° 31'.

The Former Unconquered. Symbol, an Elephant's Tusk, or, together with the next asterism, a Bed. Regents, Apas, Waters, and Visve Devas, the Combined Gods. Ruled by Venus. A severe asterism belonging to the Brahmin caste and favourable for acts of disgrace, destruction, deceit, imprisonment, beating, burning and poison when containing the Moon. Those born on the lunar day will be truthful, cleanly, wealthy, fond of fruit and flowers and sea voyages. With Moon here at birth native will be conceited, proud, constant in friendship and will have an agreeable life. Rules thatched houses and the back.

19. UTTARA ASHADHA. δ *Sagittarii.* ♐ 3° 28'.

The Latter Unconquered. Symbol and Regent the same as for the last asterism. Ruled by the Sun. A stable asterism belonging to the Kshattriya caste and favourable for coronations, expiatory ceremonies, planting of trees, sowing of seeds, building of towns, and matters of a permanent nature when containing the Moon. Those born on the lunar day will be honourable, handsome, happy, religious, fond of large animals and will be soldiers or wrestlers. With Moon here at birth native will be obedient, polite, popular, grateful and have many friends. Rules wash-houses and the hips.

20. ABHIJIT. α *Lyræ.* ♑ 14° 21′.

Victorious. Symbol, a Triangle or Three-Cornered Nut. Under its influence the Gods vanquished the Asuras. It is an asterism belonging to the Vaisya caste and is used only in horary astrology.

21. SRAVANA. α *Aquilæ.* ♒ 0° 39′.

The Ear. Symbol, a Trident. Regent, Vishnu. Ruled by the Moon. A mutable asterism belonging to the lowest caste and favourable for commencing work of an impermanent or moving character. Those born on the lunar day will be cunning, active, bold, truthful, virtuous, religious and skilful. With Moon here at birth native will be rich, learned, famous, and have a good wife. Rules parade grounds and private parts.

22. SRAVISHTHA. β *Delphini.* ♒ 15° 14′.

Most Favourable. Symbol, a Drum or Tabor. Regents, the Vasus, Bright or Good Ones. Ruled by Mars. A mutable asterism belonging to the serving caste and favourable for commencing work of an impermanent or moving character. Those born on the lunar day will be shameless, rich, generous, women haters and will have few friends. With Moon here at birth native will be wealthy, liberal, fond of music, valiant, niggardly. Rules mills and the excretory system.

23. CATABHISHAJ. λ *Aquarii.* ✕ 10° 27′.

The Hundred Physician. Regent, Varuna, goddess of the waters. Ruled by the Dragon's Head. A mutable asterism belonging to the butcher caste and favourable for commencing work of an impermanent or moving character. Those born on the lunar day will be fishermen, washermen, or dealers in wine, fish and birds. With Moon here at birth native will be eloquent, harsh in speech, truthful, adventurous, thoughtless, independent, gambler, fond of bad women, murderer of enemies. Rules streets and the right thigh.

24. PURVA BHADRA-PADA. α *Pegasi.* ✕ 22°22′.

The Former Beautiful, Auspicious, or Happy Feet. Symbol, a Couch. Regents, Aja-Ekapat, the One-footed Goat and Ahi Budhya, the Bottom Snake. Ruled by Jupiter. A severe asterism belonging to the Brahmin caste and favourable for acts of disgrace, destruction, deceit, imprisonment, beating, burning and poison when containing the Moon. Those born on the lunar day will be wicked, mean, deceitful, shepherds, thieves, torturers, and irreligious. With Moon here at birth native will be sorrowful, wealthy, clever, submissive to women, miserly and of distinct speech. Rules the southeast of houses and the left thigh.

25. UTTARA BHADRA-PADA. γ *Pegasi.* ♈ 8° 2′.

The Latter Beautiful Feet. Symbol and Regents as in the last asterism. Ruled by Saturn. A stable asterism belonging to the Kshattriya

caste and favourable for coronations, expiatory
ceremonies, planting of trees, sowing of seeds,
building of towns, and matters of a permanent
nature when containing the Moon. Those
born on the lunar day will be generous, devout,
rich, and in influential positions. With Moon here
at birth native will be happy, eloquent, charitable,
and possess children and grandchildren. Rules
swamps and the knees.

26. REVATI. *ʓ Piscium.* ♈ 18° 53′.

Rich. Symbol, a Drum or Tabor. Regent,
Pusha, the Nourisher. Ruled by Mercury. The
determinant star of this asterism marked the beginning of the celestial sphere in about 572 A.D.,
when it was 10′ west of the vernal equinox. A soft
asterism belonging to the Shudra caste and favourable for friendship, married love, purchase and making of clothes and ornaments, music and auspicious
deeds when containing the Moon. Those born on
the lunar day will be dealers in flowers, perfumes,
or ornaments and may be boatmen. With Moon
here at birth the native will be popular, a warrior,
wealthy, of strict principle, uncovetous and will have
a well-developed body. Rules flower gardens and
the ankles.

27. ASVINI. *β Arietis.* ♉ 2° 51′.

The Horsemen. Symbol, a Horse's Head. Regents, the Asvini Devas. Ruled by the Dragon's
Tail. This mansion superseded Krittika as leader
at about 400 B.C. It is a light asterism belonging

to the Vaisya caste and favourable for sales, art, sculpture, learning, marital love, wearing of ornament, medicine and purchase of carriages when containing the Moon. Those born on the lunar day will be physicians, military commanders and dealers in horses. With Moon here at birth native will be polite, fond of ornaments, handsome, popular and intelligent. Rules towns and the upper part of the feet.

28. BHARANI. 35 *Arietis.* ♉ 15° 49'.

Bearer. Regent, Yama, God of Death. Ruled by Venus. A severe asterism belonging to the lowest caste and favourable for acts of disgrace, destruction, deceit, imprisonment, beating, burning and poison when containing the Moon. Those born on the lunar day will be wicked, weak-minded, fond of killing and torture, and dealers in precious stones. With Moon here at birth native will be faithful, persevering, healthy, successful and free from cares. Rules streets and the soles of the feet.

Only 27 mansions or Nakshatras are commonly employed in Hindu astrology, Abhijit being included only in certain systems of horary astrology. When referred to the circle of the ecliptic they are made to consist of 13° 20' each, beginning with Asvini at 0° ♈. In the above descriptions the term " lunar day " refers to the day of the Full Moon that falls in the mansion.

THE CHINESE MANSIONS

1. MAO.   η *Tauri.*   ♉ 28° 52′.
The Constellation.   Ruled by the Sun.

2. PI.   α or ε *Tauri.*   ♊ 8° 40′.
A Hand-net or Rabbit-net.   Ruled by the Moon.

3. TSEE.   λ and φ *Orionis.*   ♊ 22° 35′.
The Beak or Pouting Lips.   Ruled by Mars.

4. SHEN.   δ *Orionis.*   ♊ 21° 16′.
Three Side by Side.   Ruled by Mercury.

5. TSING.   α and β *Geminorum.*   ♋ 19° 8′.
A Well or Pit.   Ruled by Jupiter.

6. KWEI.   φ with 44 M and η *Cancri.*   ♌ 6° 7′.
Spectre.   Ruled by Venus.

7. LIEU.   δ *Hydræ.*   ♌ 9° 6′.
A Willow Branch. Ruled by Saturn. This asterism governed the planets and was worshipped at the summer solstice as an emblem of immortality.

8. SING.   α *Hydræ.*   ♌ 26° 10′
A Star.   Ruled by the Sun.

9. CHANG.   ν *Hydræ.*   ♍ 5° 47′.
A Drawn Bow.   Ruled by the Moon.

10. YEN. α *Crateris*. ♍ 22° 36′.
Wings or Flanks. Ruled by Mars.

11. TCHIN. γ with β, δ, and ε *Corvi*. ♎ 9° 41′.
The Cross-piece of a Chariot. Ruled by Mercury

12. KIO. α with ζ *Virginis*. ♎ 22° 43′.
The Horn or Spike. Ruled by Jupiter.

13 KANG. κ with ι and υ *Virginis*. ♏ 3° 22′.
A Man's Neck. Ruled by Venus.

14. TI. α with β *Libræ*. ♏ 13° 58′.
Bottom. Ruled by Saturn.

15. FANG. π with β, δ, and ρ *Scorpii*. ♐ 1° 49′.
A Room or House. Ruled by the Sun. This
asterism was connected with the rearing of silkworms.

16. SIN. σ with α and τ *Scorpii*. ♐ 6° 41′.
The Heart. Ruled by the Moon.

17. WEI. μ with ε, ζ, η, θ, ι, κ, ν, and λ *Scorpii*.
♐ 15° 2′
The Tail. Ruled by Mars.

18. KI. γ with δ and ε *Sagittarii* and β *Telescopium*. ♑ 0° 9′.
A Sieve. Ruled by Mercury.

19. TOW. φ with λ and μ *Sagittarii*. ♑ 9° 1′.
A Ladle or Measure. Ruled by Jupiter.

20. NIEU. β with α, ν, ο, π, and ρ *Capricorni.*
≈≈ 2° 56'.
The Ox. Ruled by Venus. This asterism was connected with the rearing of silkworms.

21. MO. ε with μ and ν *Aquarii.* ≈≈ 10° 37'.
A Woman. Ruled by Saturn.

22. HEU. β *Aquarii.* ≈≈ 22° 17'.
Void. Ruled by the Sun.

23. GUI. α *Aquarii* with ε and θ *Pegasi.*
✕ 2° 14'.
Steep or Danger. Ruled by the Moon.

24. SHIH. α with β *Pegasi.* ✕ 22° 22'.
A House. Ruled by Mars.

25. PEIH. γ with δ *Pegasi* and α *Andromedæ.*
♈ 8° 2'.
A Wall or Partition. Ruled by Mercury.

26. GOEI. β *Andromedæ.* ♈ 29° 17'.
The Man Striding or the Striding Legs. Ruled by Jupiter.

27. LEU. β with α and γ *Arietis.* ♉ 2° 51'.
The Train of a Garment. Ruled by Venus.

28. OEI. 35 with 41, 33 and 39 *Arietis.* ♉ 15° 49'.
Belly. Ruled by Saturn.

At the earliest period the Chinese mansions or sieu began with No. 12, Kio, at the September equinox. They were grouped into four sets of seven sieu, each set forming one of the huge constellation figures into which the heavens were divided, the arrangement being as follows :

Nos.12 to 18 formed the constellation of the

			Azure Dragon.
,, 19 ,, 25	,,	,,	Black Warrior.
,, 26 ,, 4	,,	,,	White Tiger.
,, 5 ,, 11	..	.,	Red Bird.

No information as to the influence of these constellations is available.

CHAPTER IV

THE FIXED STARS IN NATAL ASTROLOGY

THE influence of the fixed stars differs from that of the planets in being much more dramatic, sudden and violent. As a rule planetary effects are gradual and operate comparatively slowly, one might almost say softly, whereas the stars appear to exercise most of their influence in sudden, hard, vehement bursts, producing tremendous effects for short periods, and, after raising the natives to a great height, dropping them suddenly and bringing a series of dramatic and unexpected disasters. In other words the fixed stars may elevate from poverty to the extreme height of fortune or *vice versa*, whereas the planets do not do so. It may be taken as a fairly well-established rule that the stars do not operate alone, except perhaps in those cases where they are situated on angles, and that their chief effect is transmitted by the planets. They seem to form an underlying basis upon which the horoscope is built, and if a planet falls upon a star its effect is greatly magnified, giving it a prominence in the life that is quite unwarranted by its mere position and aspects in the map. Cases are known to all astrologers in which a certain planet in a horoscope seems to be emphasized for no

92

apparent reason, so that it acts drastically throughout the life, and in a case such as this there is usually a fixed star in operation in the background through the planet concerned.

The extent and magnitude of the effects brought about by the stars depend upon several factors, namely, (a) apparent size, (b) celestial position, (c) nature of planet through which they operate, and (d) general nature of the horoscope.

(a) *Apparent size.* The magnitude of a star bears a definite relationship to its intensity   A 1st magnitude star is of great power, a 2nd magnitude star is appreciably weaker, and so on down the scale, the effect of the stars below the 4th magnitude being very small except in the case of clusters.

(b) *Celestial position.* The nearer a star may be to the ecliptic the greater is its power, and in the northern hemisphere a star with north declination is more powerful than one with south, the reverse holding good in the southern hemisphere. It has frequently been said that stars with great latitude cannot affect us, but it is very doubtful if this assumption is correct, and experience, particularly in the case of comets, seems to indicate that bodies in all parts of the celestial sphere are capable of exerting an influence upon the earth and its inhabitants.

(c) *Nature of planet through which they operate.* As already pointed out the fixed stars give strength and energy to the planets and modify their effects, but at the same time the nature of the planet exercises a strong controlling influence upon the result.

The greatest effect is obtained when the star and planet are both of the same nature, and in such cases the influence of the planet is raised to a vehement pitch, though at the same time the malefic effect of the star is diminished. Thus if the planet Mars fall upon a star of its own nature its power is increased ; if upon a star of the nature of Jupiter or Venus it is reduced and modified ; while if upon one of the nature of Saturn it is greatly changed. In other words if a planet falls upon a star of similar nature to its own it acquires intensity, while if upon one of contrary nature it becomes quiescent or distorted and may give a kind of sodden or dull effect to the character.

(d) *The general nature of the horoscope.* This is an important consideration and should not be forgotten. The result of the effect of a star upon a planet depends largely upon the strength or weakness of that planet in the horoscope. Thus in a map showing great ability and high position the success attained by the aid of a star will be of a more lasting nature than in one where this is not indicated. Furthermore, in all cases the fixed stars do not contradict the planetary indications. A man will not become a murderer, thief or forger merely through the effect of a star alone, and for this to take place the general nature of the map must be suitable and in harmony with such indications. The chief function of the stars is to emphasize qualities rather than to bestow them, and the exact nature and effect must be sought through the ordinary rules of astrology. Similarly in directions the action of the stars is much more potent if a planetary direction of a like nature is in force at the same time.

The fixed stars operate by position and are said to " cast no rays," or in other words their aspects are said to be ineffective and their influence to be exerted only by conjunction and parallel. As in in the case of the planets they are most powerful when in angles and weak when cadent, their effect being very marked when rising, culminating, setting or on the nadir even when alone. In such cases all 1st magnitude stars give honour and preferment, which will be lost or retained with trouble and danger if the star be of the nature of Mars, while if it be like Saturn there will be final disgrace and ruin. The particular angle occupied exerts its own modifying effect, the 10th house influencing the profession, the 7th the wife, the 4th the home, and the 1st the native himself.

The most powerful effect of a star is exercised when it is in conjunction or parallel with a planet, and a great deal of information on this will be found in the next chapter. It is usual to take the conjunction in exactly the same way as a planetary conjunction in a horoscope, that is, by the degree of ecliptic longitude affected by the star, and the parallel by its declination, and these positions are the only orthodox ones to use. It will be found, however, that the opposition is almost as powerful as the conjunction, and that the square has an undeniable influence which it will be unwise to neglect. In the case of the trines and sextiles very little effect, if any, is to be discovered, but in all probability this is due to the fact that, with the exception of the square and opposition, the aspects to the body of a star with latitude do not fall in the zodiacal degrees one would expect, as may be seen by the example given in the Appendix under Formula 8. It is a simple matter, however, to calculate the correct places in which such aspects fall and if this is done in a few cases it will soon be possible to arrive at a definite conclusion as to their power. The same difficulty is met with in the rising and setting of stars and a further reference to the Appendix will show that when the ecliptic longitude of a star is rising or setting the actual body of the star itself may be a long way above or below the horizon. This is particularly important when examining the angular effect of a star which may operate either through its ecliptic longitude or its bodily position, and also in computing primary directions, for in many cases the direction Ascendant conjunction star in mundo is impossible as it neither rises nor sets in the latitude at which the birth took place. Full details will be found in the Appendix enabling the student to determine for any latitude the zodiacal degrees with which a given star rises and sets, but there will be no necessity to calculate these unless he wishes to examine mundane angular influences and mundane primary directions.

One other point arises in connection with the action of stars and that is the " line of Right Ascension." It has been suggested that a star may operate through the degree to which its R.A. corresponds. Thus Algol in ♉ 25° 3′ has R.A. 45° 44′, which when converted directly into longitude without latitude corresponds to ♉ 18° 12′. Those who wish to experiment with this idea will find the method of converting R.A. into longitude without latitude in Formula 9 of the Appendix.

It will be noticed that all the influences described in the following chapter are expressed in terms of the radical horoscope and no allowance has been made for directions. This is done for the simple reason that the directional influences are exactly the same, the only difference being that they do not persist throughout the life. Therefore in studying the effects of directions the same delineations may be used if it is borne in mind that they are of a transitory nature and not lasting. Either primary or secondary directions may be used and both are calculated in the usual way.

It now remains only to consider the actual natures of the fixed stars and the manner of representing them. The generally accepted method of expressing the kind of influence exerted by any star is in terms of the planets of our Solar System. Thus a certain star may be " of the nature of Mars " for example, and this implies that it possesses characteristics similar to those exhibited in a horoscope by that planet. Frequently, however, two or more planets are mentioned, and in this case that one whose name is mentioned first is considered to represent the chief influence of the star. The second one denotes a kind of modifying influence, so that a star of the nature of Mars and Jupiter for example has an influence similar to that of Mars but modified by Jupiter. Thus the purely martial qualities are given an expansiveness by Jupiter, there is more optimism and good luck than would otherwise be the case, and so on, The effect is something like that of a promittor passing to the conjunction of a significator in directional astrology, the former being represented in our example by Jupiter and the latter by Mars. It will follow from this, of course, that the effect of a star of the nature of Jupiter and Mars would be somewhat different for the emphasis would in this case be upon Jupiter, and Mars would add fire and energy to the Jupiterian characteristics.

This method of classifying and describing the exact natures of the stars enables us to gain a good idea of each, and if it is combined with the sign and decanate occupied by the star, together with the planet and house through which the star is acting in any given map, we may refine our judgment of its specific effect considerably, and also estimate the way in which any other little-known star is acting, for its nature may be known from the general character of the constellation to which it belongs.

How these natures were first discovered or fixed we do not know, for Ptolemy, to whom we are indebted for them, gives no rules for their determination. That he followed some sort of rule seems certain for otherwise it is difficult to see how the fine shades of influence could be appreciated. According to Agrippa the natures of the fixed stars are known from the similarity of their colours to those of the planets, which he describes as follows :

Saturn, blue, leaden and shining ; Jupiter, citron near to paleness and clear ; Mars, red and fiery ; Sun, yellow, and when rising red, afterwards glittering ; Venus, white and shining, white in morning, reddish in evening ; Mercury, glittering ; Moon, fair : and to these might perhaps be added Uranus, bright and greenish ; and Neptune, also greenish but not so bright. This method, however, does not commend itself as a very scientific one, and it is extremely doubtful if it is that used by Ptolemy.

The general effect of the stars of any given nature in terms of natal astrology is as follows :

URANUS. Interest in occultism, electricity, aviation, antiquities ; abrupt. If rising, eccentricity gained by learning. If culminating, learned, eminent in arts and sciences, mechanical and inventive ability.

SATURN. Disgrace, ruin, calamity. If rising, grave, thoughtful, melancholy, liable to disgrace, much care and anxiety, connected with building, mines and minerals. If on 7th cusp and Moon afflicted by Saturn ruler of 7th, a slovenly wife. If culminating, trouble through old people, disgrace, trade losses, deceitful associates, rise followed by fall. With the luminaries, lean and infirm, many miseries. If afflicting Mercury, deafness.

JUPITER. If rising, sober, grave, patient, legacies, ecclesiastical preferment. If culminating, honour, glory, preferment, success in trade and in the Church.

MARS. Violent death, ultimate ruin by folly or pride. If rising, wealth, power, courage, generosity, ingenuity, rise to authority, martial success, subject to cuts, wounds, accidents, sores and injuries to the face, pains in the head and fevers. If culminating, martial eminence, success in trade and in occupations of a Mars nature. If afflicting Mercury, deafness.

VENUS. If rising, good fortune, happiness, gifts, fortunate for love and marriage, gain by legacies and inheritance. If culminating, honour and success, dealings with and help through women, success in occupations of a Venus nature.

MERCURY. If rising, honour, intellect, great learning. If culminating, business activity, gain through books and intellectual matters.

SATURN-JUPITER. Dignified, pious, conservative, acquisitive, retentive. Honour and preferment if culminating.

SATURN-MARS. Bold, cruel, heartless, adulterous, criminal, liar, loss of estates, poverty, few friends. If of 1st magnitude, rises by usury or unfair means. If culminating, bad name, rise by trade followed by disgrace and ruin.

SATURN-VENUS. Slovenly, very immoral, shameless, revolting, mean, sorrows in love. If rising, good-tempered, healthy, gain by industry and marriage. If culminating, improved health, fame by help of superiors.

SATURN-MERCURY. Profound liar, thief, blackguard, scandal and slander.

JUPITER-SATURN. Legacies, inheritance, fame, especially if rising, but foolish and unfortunate in love affairs. If culminating, honour and preferment.

JUPITER-MARS. High ambition, pride, love of power, grandeur of view, If rising, military honours. If culminating, high ecclesiastical honour, martial preferment, prosperity in business.

JUPITER-VENUS. Contented, happy disposition, honourable, philosophical mind, legal or ecclesiastical preferment, help through women. If rising or culminating, honour and riches.

JUPITER-MERCURY. Religious mind, thoughtful, philosophical, writer on religious or similar subjects.

MARS-SATURN. Malicious, thieving, merciless, fiendish, repulsive, liar, accidents, violent death. If culminating, military preferment but final disgrace.

MARS-JUPITER. Great pride, grandly liberal, commanding, cosmopolitan views. If rising or culminating, military honour and preferment.

MARS-SUN. Heroic, courageous, defiant, intrepid leader, warlike, danger to the eyes, violent death If rising, preferment to metal workers, soldiers, surgeons, and other Mars people. If culminating, preferment in business and in all martial affairs.

MARS-VENUS. Strong passions, artistic feeling, gain through women and friends, honour and preferment in martial affairs, especially if rising or culminating.

MARS-MERCURY. High enterprise, combative, destructive. If rising, rash, very obstinate, ruined by headstrong and precipitate conduct. If culminating, changeable in business.

MARS-MOON. Adventurous, perfidious, insolent, wanton, brutal, danger to eyes. If rising, sore eyes, weak sight, trouble and loss through women. If culminating, disgrace and imprisonment.

SUN-MARS. Fearless, intolerant, warlike skill, over-confident, fierce, cruel, vindictive, energetic organizer, danger to the eyes, accidents, violent death.

VENUS-SATURN. Cunning, bad morals, mercenary, repulsive habits, perverted tastes, unfortunate love affairs, seduction.

VENUS-JUPITER. Refined, good, high morals, vivacious, sincere, pure, healthy, artistic, fortunate in love and marriage, help through relatives.

VENUS-MARS. Shameless, vain, self-indulgent, abandoned, violent passions, danger of seduction, riotous living but often self-respecting and decent.

VENUS-MERCURY. Idealistic, psychic, handsome, neat, lovable, refined, genteel, intelligent.

MERCURY-SATURN. Subtle, studious, keen and profound mind, often shameless liar, interested in occult or serious subjects.

MERCURY-JUPITER. Optimistic, cheerful, philosophical, broad mind, religious views, success through influential friends or the Church and law.

MERCURY-MARS. Exaggerative, argumentative, unreliable, unscrupulous, given to invective, mechanical ability, very quick mind, great talker.

MERCURY-VENUS. Courteous, affable, orderly, elegant, sweet-tempered, lovable, refined, artistic, honour and riches, If rising, love of poetry, painting and teaching, quick mind. If culminating, success in literary and legal professions.

MOON-MARS. Changeable, passionate, wanton, liable to accidents especially when travelling, bad eyes, injuries to face.

NEBULÆ AND CLUSTERS. Blindness, disease, accidents, fevers, quarrels, rape, murder, banishment and decapitation.

No difficulty should be experienced in using the fixed stars in natal astrology, but for the benefit of the beginner the following rules may be laid down :

1. Note on the map or make a list of the fixed stars that fall in conjunction and parallel with, or in opposition to, the planets, together with their magnitudes and natures. The following orbs may be allowed for conjunction and opposition : For a 1st magnitude star, 7° 30'; for a 2nd magnitude, 5° 30'; for a 3rd magnitude, 3° 40' ; and for a 4th magnitude, 1° 30'

2. Look up the constellation containing the star, its nature as tabulated above, and the combined influence of star and planet as given in the next chapter.

3. Modify these characteristics by the sign, decanate and house occupied, together with the aspects to the planet and the houses it rules just as would be done in the case of an ordinary planetary conjunction.

4. The magnitude of the star and its angular, succeedent or cadent position will give some idea of the strength likely to be exhibited.

As an example we may take the horoscope of the

ex-Kaiser, who was born at Berlin on 27 January, 1859, at 3 p.m. The chief positions are as follows : Ascendant conjunction Pollux, M.C. and Neptune conjunction Markab, Mars conjunction Scheat, Uranus conjunction, and Moon opposition, Pleiades, and Mercury conjunction Wega.

The most striking position is Markab, a 2nd magnitude Mars-Mercury star in Pegasus on the M.C. and in conjunction with Neptune and Mars. This star brings disgrace and ruin, and with Neptune gives a romantic, emotional and unbalanced mind, while the constellation Pegasus gives vanity, ambition and bad judgment—a disastrous attempt to find " a place in the Sun " if one may apply the legend literally. The nature of the star is combative, destructive and aggressive, and its particular mode of operation is greatly influenced by Mars conjunction Neptune afflicted by Sun and Saturn, which indicates martial megalomania and downfall. We should, therefore, expect these characteristics to be tremendously emphasized and matters connected with them to end in a crash of a far greater magnitude than Mars conjunction Neptune would indicate alone.

Furthermore, Pollux, a martial star, is rising, indicating imprisonment and honour of short duration, while the Moon is heavily afflicted by Uranus from the Pleiades giving deformity (the ex-Kaiser has a paralysed arm) and heavy losses at the end of life, together in such a case as this with revolutions and popular outbreaks caused by Uranus falling on a star of the nature of the Moon and Mars.

At the outbreak of the war in 1914, the Kaiser's

Sun was separating from Difda, and Mars from Hamal and the Ascendant was in conjunction with Regulus. The last position is a very significant one indicating military honour and success but ultimate failure. Difda also denotes self-destruction by brute-force, while Hamal is a violent and destructive star of the nature of Mars and Saturn, which with Mars gives final disgrace and ruin.

Another interesting study is that of the Emperor Franz Josef of Austria, whose life was a succession of disasters, many of which were due to the position of the Sun, Moon and Saturn in conjunction with Alphard in the neck of the Hydra, but examples could be multiplied indefinitely and the student will soon discover for himself that the use of the fixed stars and constellations is indeed a valuable help to the understanding of a horoscope.

CHAPTER V

THE INFLUENCE OF FIXED STARS, NEBULÆ AND CLUSTERS

In the following Table will be found the names and positions of all the stars, nebulæ and clusters that have been mentioned in astrological literature, arranged in order of longitude and corrected up to 1st January, 1920.

A rough and ready means of determining their positions for any other year is to add $50\frac{1}{4}''$ per annum to their longitudes if the year is after 1920, and to subtract that amount for each year before 1920. Thus if the positions are required for, say, 1887, which is 33 years before 1920, all that must be done is to multiply $50\frac{1}{4}''$ by 33 and subtract the result, namely, $1658''$ or $27' 38''$ from the longitude given in the Table; whilst if the positions were required for 1953, or 33 years later, the same amount would have to be added. The latitudes do not vary to any appreciable extent from year to year.

This will be found sufficient for all ordinary purposes, but if greater accuracy is required it may be obtained by employing Right Ascension and Declination. Two columns will be found giving the Annual Variation in R.A. and Dec. for each star. This quantity must be multiplied by the number of years between the required date and 1920, and then added to or subtracted from the R.A. and Dec. given in the Tables. The correct position can then be calculated by the use of Formula 5 in the Appendix. In the case of R.A. the annual variation is always to be added if the year for which the positions are required is later than 1920, and subtracted if earlier. In the case of Dec., however, if the annual variation is positive it means that the star is travelling northwards and therefore for years later than 1920 it must be added for stars with North Dec. and subtracted for those with South Dec., and vice versa if earlier than 1920. Conversely if the annual variation is negative the star is travelling southwards and the correction must be subtracted for stars with North Dec., and added for those with South Dec. if after 1920, and vice versa if before. The positions of many of the stars, however, are given yearly in the *Nautical Almanac, Whitaker's Almanac,* and other similar publications, and a reference to these will give the R.A. and Dec. without the trouble of correction.

In any case never use the Tables of star positions given in the old astrological works, and for that matter in most modern ones, for they are very incorrect. For example, Vindemiatrix, which is in the first decanate of Libra, is given by Wilson, Simmonite, and Alvidas as in the beginning of Virgo, and a multitude of similar, though perhaps not so glaring errors might easily be mentioned. In the present case every care has been taken to compute the positions accurately and they have all been carefully checked, so that the possibility of error is very remote.

1930 + 11'   1960 44'
1940 +22'   1970 55
1950 + 33   1980 1° 6'

POSITIONS OF THE CHIEF STARS, NEBUL

No.	Name	Cat. Name	Mag.	Nature	Long
					°
162 1	Difda	β Ceti	2	♄	♈ 1
122 2	Algenib	γ Pegasi	3	♂ ☿	8
133 3	Alpheratz	α Andromedæ	2	♃ ♀	13
145 4	Baten Kaitos	ζ Ceti	3½	♄	20
134 5	Al Pherg	η Piscium	4	♄ ♃	25
214 6	Vertex	31 M Andromedæ	N	♂ ☽	26
178 7	Mirach	β Andromedæ	2	♀	29
207 8	Sharatan	β Arietis	3	♂ ♄	♉ 2
170 9	Hamal	α Arietis	2	♂ ♄	6
128 10	Almach	γ Andromedæ	2	♀	13
176 11	Menkar	α Ceti	2½	♄	13
154 12	Capulus	33 H vi Persei	C	♂ ☿	23
123 13	Algol	β Persei	V	♄ ♃	25
108 14	Alcyone	η Tauri	3	☽ ♂	28
188 15	Prima Hyadum	γ Tauri	4	♄ ☿	♊ 4
119 16	Aldebaran	α Tauri	1	♂	8
197 17	Rigel	β Orionis	1	♃ ♂	15
145 18	Bellatrix	γ Orionis	2	♂ ☿	19
151 19	Capella	α Aurigæ	1	♂ ☿	20
181 20	Phact	α Columbæ	2	♀ ☿	21
177 21	Mintaka	δ Orionis	2	♄ ☿	21
164 22	El Nath	β Tauri	2	♂	21
165 23	Ensis	42 M Orionis	N	♂ ☽	21
128 24	Alnilam	ε Orionis	2	♃ ♄	22
125 25	Al Hecka	ζ Tauri	3	♂	23
184 26	Polaris	α Ursæ Minoris	2	♄ ♀	27

ND CLUSTERS FOR 1st JAN., 1920.

Lat.			R.A.			Ann. Var.	Decl.				Ann. Var.
	°	′	°	′	″	′		°	′	″	″
S	20	46	9	53	37·0	+45·1	S	18	24	52·4	+19·8
N	12	36	2	16	42·6	46·3	N	14	44	19·6	20·0
N	25	41	1	3	43·8	46·5	N	28	38	35·6	19·9
S	20	20	26	52	39·7	44·4	S	10	43	47·4	17·8
N	5	22	21	47	59·2	48·1	N	14	56	1·6	18·6
N	33	21	9	34	22·5	48·4	N	40	49	55·0	19·7
N	25	56	16	18	42·4	50·2	N	35	11	48·4	19·1
N	8	29	27	33	14·8	49·6	N	20	25	3·1	17·7
N	9	58	30	39	53·1	50·7	N	23	5	5·3	17·1
N	27	48	29	44	42·9	55·0	N	41	56	47·2	17·3
S	12	35	44	31	25·6	46·9	N	3	46	35·9	14·2
N	40	22	33	20	45·0	61·8	N	56	46	54·0	16·8
N	22	25	45	44	21·1	58·6	N	40	38	54·4	14·0
N	4	2	55	40	52·9	53·4	N	23	51	31·5	11·3
S	5	44	63	48	34·5	51·1	N	15	26	7·6	8·8
S	5	28	67	49	55·2	51·6	N	16	20	58·3	7·4
S	31	8	77	40	23·1	43·2	S	8	17	35·2	4·3
S	16	50	80	12	35·5	48·3	N	6	16	41·5	3·4
N	22	55	77	41	38·7	66·4	N	45	55	5·1	3·8
S	57	23	84	11	16·2	32·5	S	34	6	58·1	2·0
S	23	37	81	58	46·8	45·9	S	0	21	26·5	2·8
N	5	23	80	18	30·1	56·8	N	28	32	28·1	3·2
S	28	42	82	53	0·0	47·7	S	5	26	27·0	2·7
S	24	32	83	2	18·0	45·6	S	1	15	7·3	2·4
S	2	12	83	12	56·5	53·8	N	21	5	41·7	2·3
N	66	5	22	55	18·1	450·6	N	88	52	38·9	18·4

No.	Name	Cat. Name	Mag.	Nature	Long
					°
146 27	Betelgeuze	α Orionis	1	♂ ☿	27
175 28	Menkalinan	β Aurigæ	2	♂ ☿	28
213 29	Tejat	η Geminorum	3	☿ ♀	♋ 2
163 30	Dirah	μ Geminorum	3	☿ ♀	4
126 31	Alhena	γ Geminorum	2	☿ ♀	7
208 32	Sirius	α Canis Majoris	1	♃ ♂	12
150 33	Canopus	α Argus	1	♄ ♃	13
216 34	Wasat	δ Geminorum	3	♄	17
193 35	Propus	ι Geminorum	4	☿ ♀	17
154 36	Castor	α Geminorum	2	☿	19
185 37	Pollux	β Geminorum	1	♂	22
191 38	Procyon	α Canis Minoris	1	☿ ♂	24
187 39	Præsæpe	44 M Cancri	C	♂ ☽	♌ 6
142 40	North Asellus	γ Cancri	5	♂ ☉	6
143 41	South Asellus	δ Cancri	4	♂ ☉	7
116 42	Acubens	α Cancri	4	♄ ☿	12
123 43	Algenubi	ε Leonis	3	♄ ♂	19
130 44	Alphard	α Hydræ	2	♄ ♀	26
117 45	Adhafera	ζ Leonis	3	♄ ☿	26
128 46	Al Jabhah	η Leonis	3	♄ ☿	26
199 47	Regulus	α Leonis	1	♂ ♃	28
219 48	Zosma	δ Leonis	2	♄ ♀	♍ 10
160 49	Denebola	β Leonis	2	♄ ♀	20
157 50	Copula	51 M Canum Ven.	N	☽ ♀	23
173 51	Labrum	δ Crateris	4	♀ ☿	25
219 52	Zavijava	β Virginis	3½	☿ ♂	26
174 53	Markeb	κ Argus	2½	♄ ♃	27
218 54	Zaniah	η Virginis	4	☿ ♀	♎ 3
214 55	Vindemiatrix	ε Virginis	3	♄ ☿	8

Lat.			R.A.			Ann. Var.	Decl.				Ann. Var.
°	′		°	′	″	″		°	′	″	″
S	16	2	87	42	36·3	+48·7	N	7	23	35·9	+ 0·8
N	21	30	88	24	54·6	66·0	N	44	56	26·7	+ 0·5
S	0	54	92	30	43·9	54·3	N	22	31	52·4	− 0·9
S	0	50	94	31	49·2	54·4	N	22	33	21·2	1·7
S	6	45	98	16	21·9	52·0	N	16	28	7·3	2·9
S	39	35	100	24	22·0	39·6	S	16	36	19·9	4·8
S	75	50	95	32	37·3	18·3	S	52	39	5·5	1·9
S	0	11	108	50	12·4	53·6	N	22	7	51·1	6·5
N	5	45	110	11	24·4	55·9	N	27	57	29·8	7·0
N	10	5	112	22	26·8	57·4	N	32	3	55·9	7·7
N	6	40	115	6	21·0	55·2	N	28	13	14·9	8·6
S	16	0	113	46	43·6	47·1	N	5	25	51·8	9·1
N	1	33	128	54	15·0	51·6	N	20	15	8·0	12·2
N	3	11	129	40	1·0	52·3	N	21	45	43·3	12·5
N	0	4	130	2	7·3	51·1	N	18	26	57·1	13·1
S	5	5	133	31	42·9	49·2	N	12	10	5·6	13·8
N	9	43	145	19	42·4	51·1	N	24	8	35·7	16·5
S	22	23	140	54	51·1	44·2	S	8	18	40·2	15·5
N	11	52	153	3	39·9	50·1	N	23	48	59·5	17·9
N	4	52	150	44	36·3	49·0	N	17	9	11·9	17·5
N	0	28	151	1	42·3	48·0	N	12	21	31·3	17·5
N	14	20	167	27	50·8	47·8	N	20	57	44·0	19·7
N	12	16	176	14	42·4	45·9	N	15	1	9·6	20·1
N	50	55	201	35	37·5	36·7	N	47	36	18·0	18·6
S	17	34	168	50	5·5	34·5	S	14	20	43·6	19·5
N	0	42	176	37	55·3	46·9	N	2	12	56·0	20·3
S	63	43	139	54	31·3	27·9	S	54	40	6·8	15·3
N	1	22	183	57	11·1	46·0	S	0	13	20·4	20·0
N	16	13	194	32	55·2	+44·8	N	11	23	19·8	~19·4

	No.	Name	Cat. Name	Mag.	Nature	Long.
						°
153	56	Caphir	γ Virginis	3½	☿ ♀	9
125	57	Algorab	δ Corvi	3	♂ ♄	12
207	58	Seginus	γ Boötis	3	☿ ♄	16
167	59	Foramen	η Argus	V	♄ ♃	21
211	60	Spica	α Virginis	1	♀ ♂	22
139	61	Arcturus	α Boötis	1	♂ ♃	23
190	62	Princeps	δ Boötis	3	☿ ♄	♏ 2
173	63	Khambalia	λ Virginis	4	☿ ♂	5
116	64	Acrux	α Crucis	1	♃	10
131	65	Alphecca	α Coronæ Bor.	2	♀ ☿	11
205	66	South Scale	α Libræ	3	♃ ♂	13
203	67	North Scale	β Libræ	2½	♃ ☿	18
213	68	Unukalhai	α Serpentis	2½	♄ ♂	20
117	69	Agena	β Centauri	1	♀ ♃	22
148	70	Bungula	α Centauri	1	♀ ♃	28
218	71	Yed Prior	δ Ophiuchi	3	♄ ♀	♐ 1
172	72	Isidis	δ Scorpii	2	♂ ♄	1
169	73	Graffias	β Scorpii	3	♂ ♄	2
171	74	Han	ζ Ophiuchi	3	♄ ♀	8
136	75	Antares	α Scorpii	1	♂ ♃	8
194	76	Rastaban	β Draconis	3	♄ ♀	10
199	77	Sabik	η Ophiuchi	2	♄ ♀	16
193	78	Rasalhague	α Ophiuchi	2	♄ ♀	21
173	79	Lesath	υ Scorpii	3	☿ ♂	22
117	80	Aculeus	6 M Scorpii	C	♂ ☽	24
117	81	Acumen	7 M Scorpii	C	♂ ☽	27
208	82	Sinistra	ν Ophiuchi	3	♄ ♀	28
212	83	Spiculum	8, 20, 21 M Sagittarii	CNC.	♂ ☽	29
185	84	Polis	μ Sagittarii	4	♃ ♂	♑ 2

o.	Lat.			R.A.			Ann. Var.	Decl.			Ann Var.
		°	′	°	′	″	″		°	′	″	″
6	N	2	48	189	24	5·1	+45·6	S	1	0	39·2	−19·8
7	S	12	11	186	25	50·2	46·5	S	16	4	12·7	20·1
8	N	49	33	217	12	51·6	36·3	N	38	39	27·3	15·8
9	S	58	55	160	29	11·8	57·3	S	59	15	40·6	18·7
0	S	2	3	200	14	38·4	47·4	S	10	44	39·0	18·8
1	N	30	47	213	0	10·6	41·1	N	19	35	54·0	18·8
2	N	48	59	228	4	9·7	36·3	N	33	36	45·1	13·5
3	N	0	28	213	36	39·0	47·8	S	13	0	19·6	16·6
4	S	52	52	185	32	7·6	49·8	S	62	39	22·5	20·0
5	N	44	20	232	49	30·3	38·1	N	26	58	59·2	12·2
6	N	0	20	221	36	44·2	49·6	S	15	42	36·6	15·1
7	N	8	30	228	10	29·5	48·4	S	9	5	19·2	13·4
8	N	25	25	235	4	53·5	44·2	N	6	40	35·1	11·4
9	S	44	9	209	32	27·7	63·1	S	59	59	15·3	17·5
0	S	42	34	218	32	18·1	60·9	S	60	30	21·8	15·0
1	N	17	15	242	32	16·2	47·1	S	3	29	21·9	9·4
2	S	1	58	238	53	59·7	53·1	S	22	23	42·7	10·4
3	N	1	1	240	11	43·8	52·2	S	19	35	15·4	10·0
4	N	11	24	248	11	16·6	49·5	S	10	24	22·2	7·4
5	S	4	34	246	7	29·1	55·0	S	26	15	20·4	8·1
6	N	75	17	262	9	21·9	20·2	N	52	21	36·2	2·7
7	N	7	12	256	26	49·3	51·6	S	15	37	37·4	4·6
8	N	35	51	262	48	18·0	41·7	N	12	37	1·9	2·7
9	S	14	0	261	19	48·6	61·0	S	37	14	0·0	3·1
0	S	8	50	263	44	42·0	58·3	S	32	9	46·0	2·3
1	S	11	22	267	7	12·0	59·8	S	34	47	22·0	1·1
2	N	13	41	268	39	19·5	49·5	S	9	45	53·7	0·6
3	N	0	1	269	30	—	54·5	S	23	26	—	− 0·4
4	N	2	21	272	14	40·8	+53·6	S	21	4	51·7	+ 0·8

	No.	Name	Cat. Name	Mag.	Nature	Long.	
						°	
165	85	Facies	22 M Sagittarii	C	☉ ♂	7	1.
180	86	Pelagus	σ Sagittarii	2	♃ ☿	11	1
141	87	Ascella	ζ Sagittarii	3	♃ ☿	12	3
173	88	Manubrium	o Sagittarii	4½	☉ ♂	13	5
185	89	Wega	α Lyræ	1	♀ ☿	14	1
158	90	Deneb	ζ Aquilæ	3	♂ ♃	18	4
213	91	Terebellum	ω Sagittarii	6	♀ ♄	24	4
118	92	Albireo	β Cygni	3	♀ ☿	♒ 0	
135	93	Altair	α Aquilæ	1	♂ ♃	0	3
167	94	Giedi	α Capricorni	4	♀ ♂	2	4
157	95	Dabih	β Capricorni	3	♄ ♀	2	5
180	96	Oculus	π Capricorni	5	♄ ♀	3	3
148	97	Bos	ρ Capricorni	5	♄ ♀	4	
141	98	Armus	η Capricorni	5	♂ ☿	11	3
163	99	Dorsum	θ Capricorni	5	♄ ♃	12	4
156	100	Castra	ε Capricorni	5	♄ ♃	19	
179	101	Nashira	γ Capricorni	4	♄ ♃	20	4
202	102	Sadalsuud	β Aquarii	3	♄ ☿	22	1
159	103	Deneb Algedi	δ Capricorni	3	♄ ♃	22	2
200	104	Sadalmelik	α Aquarii	3	♄ ☿	♓ 2	1
165	105	Fomalhaut	α Piscis Aust.	1	♀ ☿	2	4
159	106	Deneb Adige	α Cygni	1	♀ ☿	4	1
210	107	Skat	δ Aquarii	3	♄ ♃	7	4
116	108	Achernar	α Eridani	1	♃	14	1
174	109	Markab	α Pegasi	2	♂ ☿	22	2
206	110	Scheat	β Pegasi	2	♂ ☿	28	1

No.	Lat.			R.A.			Ann. Var.	Decl.			Ann. Var.
		°	′		°	′	″	″		°	′	″	″
85	S	0	43	277	52	37·5	+54·7	S	23	58	0·0	+2·4
86	S	3	26	282	34	34·8	55·8	S	26	23	50·6	4·3
87	S	7	10	284	22	50·2	57·3	S	29	59	44·3	5·0
88	N	0	52	284	58	21·5	53·6	S	21	51	45·0	5·2
89	N	61	44	278	33	26·7	30·4	N	38	42	30·3	3·3
90	N	36	12	285	25	59·5	41·4	N	13	44	36·6	5·2
91	S	5	25	297	43	46·5	54·7	S	26	31	13·3	9·2
92	N	48	59	291	52	25·2	36·3	N	27	47	26·8	7·5
93	N	29	18	296	43	12·0	43·9	N	8	39	21·9	9·4
94	N	6	58	303	21	16·4	49·9	S	12	46	34·4	11·0
95	N	4	36	304	7	46·2	50·5	S	15	2	5·9	11·3
96	N	0	54	305	41	15·1	51·4	S	18	28	34·9	11·5
97	N	1	12	306	4	29·4	51·3	S	18	4	44·6	11·8
98	S	2	59	314	57	55·3	51·1	S	20	10	27·9	14·1
99	S	0	36	315	22	6·0	50·4	S	17	34	8·1	14·0
00	S	4	58	323	9	10·6	50·4	S	19	49	36·3	15·9
01	S	2	33	323	54	54·9	49·9	S	17	1	27·5	16·2
02	N	8	37	321	50	13·8	47·4	S	5	55	25·7	15·8
03	S	2	35	325	39	24·6	49·6	S	16	29	27·6	16·3
04	N	10	39	330	25	8·1	46·2	S	0	42	32·7	17·4
05	S	21	8	343	18	29·5	49·8	S	30	2	47·5	19·0
06	N	59	55	309	40	33·7	30·6	N	44	59	37·7	12·8
07	S	8	11	342	36	5·5	47·8	S	16	14	47·8	19·1
08	S	59	22	23	41	3·6	33·6	S	57	38	34·5	18·3
09	N	19	24	345	11	36·9	44·8	N	14	46	28·2	19·3
10	N	31	8	344	58	24·3	+43·6	N	27	38	54·7	+19·5

In the following pages will be found a description of the influence of each star in as much detail as could be obtained. The stars are arranged alphabetically to facilitate reference, and the longitude is also added in each case to enable the position in the Table to be found without trouble.

1. ACHERNAR. α *Eridani.* ♓ 14° 10'.
Notes. A white star situated at the mouth of the River. From Al Ahir al Nahr, the End of the River.
Influence. In his notes on the stars in Eridanus Ptolemy says " the last bright one is of the same influence as Jupiter." It is symbolized as the Cherub and Sword and gives success in public office, beneficence, and religion.

2. ACRUX. α *Crucis.* ♏ 10° 46'
Notes. The brightest star in the Southern Cross. It is triple.
Influence. Acrux is of the nature of Jupiter. It gives religious beneficence, ceremonial, justice, magic and mystery, and is frequently prominent in the horoscopes of astrologers and occultists.

3. ACUBENS. α *Cancri.* ♌ 12° 31'.
Notes. A double star with white and red components situated on the southern claw of the Crab. From Al Zubanah, the Claws.
Influence. Of the nature of Saturn and Mercury. It has been called " The sheltering or hiding place," and gives activity, malevolence and poison, making its natives liars and criminals.

4. ACULEUS. 6M *Scorpii.* ♐ 24° 39'.

Notes. The so-called Nebula in the sting of Scorpio mentioned by Ptolemy. It is actually a cluster and lies with Acumen a little above the sting.

Influence. Of the nature of Mars and the Moon. It affects the eyesight and causes blindness of one or both eyes if in conjunction with an afflicted luminary, or in conjunction with a malefic that afflicts the luminaries. The opposition appears to be equally effective.

5. ACUMEN. 7M *Scorpii.* ♐ 27° 35'.

Notes. A companion cluster to Aculeus and of the same nature and influence.

6. ADHAFERA. ζ *Leonis.* ♌ 26° 27'.

Notes. A double star in the Lion's mane. It has been called Al Serpha, the Funeral Pyre.

Influence. Of the nature of Saturn and Mercury. It is connected with suicide, poison, corrosive acids, liquid explosives, liquid fire, lying, stealing and crime.

If rising gives great military preferment and riches.

7 AGENA. β *Centauri.* ♏ 22° 43'.

Notes. On the right foreleg of the Centaur.

Influence. According to Ptolemy it is of the nature of Venus and Jupiter, but Alvidas suggests an influence similar to that of Mars conjunction Mercury. It gives position, friendship, refinement, morality, health and honour.

With Sun. Mental activity, rashness, success, many friendships.

With Moon. Sarcasm and bitter speech, strong passions.

With Mercury. Great mental ability, sarcasm, material gain, speaking, writing and championing the masses.

With Venus. Poetical, strong passions, rash friendships with women.

With Mars. Legal authority, honour as speaker or writer, great mental and physical powers.

With Jupiter. Intellectual success, legal and Church authority, professional honour.

With Saturn. Thoughtful, shrewd, association with medical men, healing powers, abrupt manner, occultism, domestic disharmony through jealousy.

With Uranus. Sarcasm, public work but eventual disfavour of superiors, caustic speaker and writer, violent, coarse, unrefined, strong passions, domestic disharmony, loss of expected wealth, peculiar death.

With Neptune. Sharp, rash, headstrong, original, organizer, poor executive ability, loss through law and speculation, obstacles to success, many false friends and enemies, liable to accidents, death by colds or fevers.

8. ALBIREO. *β Cygni.* ♒ 0° 9′.

Notes. A topaz yellow and sapphire blue binary or double star situated on the head of the Swan. Symbolized as " The Song of the Dying Swan."

Influence. Of the nature of Venus and Mercury.

It gives a handsome appearance, neatness, a lovable disposition and beneficence in despair.

9. ALCYONE. η *Tauri.* ♉ 28° 52′.

Legend. Alcyone represents the Pleiad, daughter of Atlas and Pleione, who became the mother of Hyrieus by Neptune.

Notes. A greenish yellow star and brightest of the Pleiades, situated on the shoulder of the Bull. From early times it has been thought to be the central Sun round which the universe revolves, and was Al Wasat, the Central One, of the Arabs, and Temennu, the Foundation Stone, of the Babylonians, but this idea has now been abandoned by astronomers. Alcyone marked the beginning of the 4th ecliptic constellation of the Babylonians, and as Amba, the Mother, formed the junction star between the Hindu nakshatras Krittika and Rohini. It is frequently called the Hen.

Influence. Of the nature of Mars and the Moon. It causes love, eminence, blindness from fevers, small-pox, and accidents to the face. For further particulars see PLEIADES.

10. ALDEBARAN. α *Tauri.* ♊ 8° 40′.

Notes. A pale rose star marking the Bull's South or Left Eye. Its name is from Al Dabaran, the Follower. It formed one of the four Royal Stars or Watchers of the Heavens among the Persians in about 3000 B.C., when, as the Watcher of the East, it marked the Vernal Equinox, the other stars being Regulus, Antares, and Fomalhaut. Aldebaran is a star of the Solar Spectrum type distant from us about 28 light years and receding at the rate of about 30 miles a second.

Influence. According to Ptolemy it is of the nature of Mars, but Alvidas states that it is similar to Mercury, Mars and Jupiter conjoined. It gives honour, intelligence, eloquence, steadfastness, integrity, popularity, courage, ferocity, a tendency to sedition, a responsible position, public honours and gain of power and wealth through others, but its benefits seldom prove lasting and there is also danger of violence and sickness.

If culminating. Honour, preferment, good fortune and favours from women.

If rising, and in conjunction with the Moon, a good fellow, but if in conjunction with both the lord of the Ascendant and the Moon it denotes a murderer, especially if the lord of the Ascendant is a masculine planet and the Sun is at the same time afflicted.

With Sun. Great energy and perseverance, high material honours but danger of losing them, danger from quarrels and the law, honour and riches ending in disgrace and ruin, liable to disease, fevers and a violent death. If in conjunction with both Sun and Mars, great liability to pestilential fevers.

With Moon. Favourable for business, honour and credit, especially if in the 1st or 10th house, but danger of calamity. Favourable for domestic, public and religious matters; danger of a violent death. If at the same time Mars or Saturn is with Antares the native is liable to be hanged or killed by a sword thrust.

With Sun or Moon, culminating or rising, great honour through violence with difficulties and casualties.

With Mercury. Affects the health and domestic affairs, prominence through mercurial matters, material gain, and many learned friends.

With Venus. Honour through literature, music or art ; creative abilities ; favourable for health and marriage.

With Mars. Great military preferment but attended by much danger ; liable to accidents, fevers and a violent death. If at the same time the Moon is with Antares, especially in an angle, death will come through a stab, blow or fall.

With Jupiter. Great ecclesiastical honour and high military preferment.

With Saturn. Great afflictions, strange mind, great wickedness, sarcasm, eloquence, good memory, studious and retiring nature, legal abilities, domestic and material success, losses through mercurial friends. If at the same time the Moon is with Antares there will be a violent death, probably by hanging.

With Uranus. Scientific, a nature lover, critical, just, domestic and political success, public honours, fond of occultism but may meet with disfavour through it, lingering death.

With Neptune. Connected with science, art, occultism and mediumship, good intellect, loss through fire, electricity or speculation, but gain through metals, machinery or scientific instruments, especially if Mars is strong ; many journeys, obstacles to domestic happiness, unfavourable for children, danger of accidents and sudden death.

With Fortuna or its dispositor, poverty.

With a malefic in the 4th, 7th, 11th or 12th house and the Moon at the same time with Antares, death by a sudden sword thrust, stab or fall.

11. ALGENIB. γ *Pegasi.* ♈ 8° 2′.

Notes. A white star situated at the tip of the wing of Pegasus. From Al Janah, the Wing, or Al Janb, the Side. According to Bullinger it means " Who carries."

Influence. Of the nature of Mars and Mercury It gives notoriety, dishonour, violence, misfortune, and denotes the naked and poor professional beggar.

With Sun. Mental disturbances, fevers and ill-health, some danger of accidents.

With Moon. Dishonour, loss by scandal, exiled or forced to flee, ill-health, trouble through writings.

With Mercury. Quick temper, mental disturbances, success in legal and other disputes.

With Venus. Generous, proud, quick temper, bad morals, drink or evil habits, favourable for financial affairs.

With Mars. Quick mind and body, lying or theft, danger of accidents.

With Jupiter. Hypocrisy, financial success, real or pretended religious enthusiasm.

With Saturn. Many enemies, success, secret help from powerful friends and influential relatives, bad morals.

With Uranus. Active and eccentric mind, reformer or agitator, great influence over the minds of others necessitating journeys, peculiar ideas in advance of the times, mystic and fond of mysteries though frank and open, domestic troubles especially in a woman's map.

With Neptune. Conceited, stubborn, deceptive, cowardly, vacillating, untruthful, envious, superstitious, strong passions, sex troubles, evil surroundings, many enemies, mechanical ability, criminal tendencies, may be forger, sudden and violent death.

12. ALGENUBI. ϵ *Leonis.* ♌ 19° 35'.

Notes. A yellow star in the Lion's mouth.

Influence. Of the nature of Saturn and Mars, and has been called " He who rends." It gives a bold, bombastic, cruel, heartless, brutish and destructive nature, but artistic appreciation and power of expression.

13. ALGOL. β *Persei.* ♉ 25° 3'.

Legend. Algol represents the head of the Gorgon Medusa who was slain by Perseus. Medusa, who was the only mortal one of the three Gorgon sisters, was originally a beautiful maiden, but her hair was changed into hissing serpents by Minerva in consequence of her having become by Neptune the mother of Chrysaor and Pegasus in one of Minerva's temples. This gave her so fearful an appearance that everyone who looked at her was changed into stone.

Notes. A white binary and variable star marking the Medusa's Head held in the hand of Perseus. Its diameter is 1,060,000 miles, and its density only a little above that of cork. Algol is from Ra's al Ghul, the Demon's Head, other names in frequent use being Caput Algol and Caput Medusæ. It was known as Lilith by the Hebrews, after the nocturnal vampire said to be Adam's first wife ; and Tseih She, Piled-up Corpses, by the Chinese.

Influence. Of the nature of Saturn and Jupiter. It causes misfortune, violence, decapitation, hanging, electrocution and mob violence, and gives a dogged and violent nature that causes death to the native or others. It is the most evil star in the heavens.

If culminating. Murder, sudden death, beheading, prone to murder and mischief. If at the same time in conjunction with Sun, Moon or Jupiter, gives victory over others in war.

With Sun. Violent death or extreme sickness. If also in no aspect to a benefic, or there is no benefic in the 8th house, and the dispositor of the Sun in a day nativity or of the Moon in the night one is in square or opposition to Mars, the native will be beheaded ; if the luminary culminate he will be maimed, mangled, wounded or torn to pieces alive ; and if Mars is at the same time in Gemini or Pisces his hands or feet will be cut off.

With Moon. Violent death or extreme sickness.

With Mars, or if Mars be elevated above the luminaries when Algol is angular, the native will be a murderer who will come to an untimely end. The same is caused by Algol angular or with the hyleg.

With Mars or Saturn, and the Moon at the same time with Sadalmelik, hanging or decapitation by royal command ; if the Moon is with Denebola, death by judicial sentence ; and, if the Moon is with Alphard, death by water or poison.

With the Hyleg and angular, decapitation **or a** murderer who meets with a violent death.

With Fortuna or its dispositor, poverty.

14. ALGORAB. δ *Corvi* ♎ 12° 20'.
Notes. A double star, pale yellow and purple, situated on the right wing of the Crow. From Al Ghirab, the Crow.
Influence. Of the nature of Mars and Saturn. It gives destructiveness, malevolence, fiendishness, repulsiveness and lying, and is connected with scavenging.

15. AL HECKA. ζ *Tauri.* ♊ 23° 40'.
Notes. The Bull's South or Following Horn. sometimes called " The Driver."
Influence. According to Ptolemy it is of the nature of Mars, but Alvidas suggests that of Mercury and Saturn conjoined. It gives violence, malevolence and danger of accidents.
With Sun. Suspicious, reserved, studious, unfavourable for health and especially for the lungs, aptitude for military enterprise and stratagems but danger of deceit and ambushes.
With Moon. Quarrels, evil habits and company, depravity.
With Mercury. Hasty temper, selfishness, greed, dissipation, legal and business troubles, poor health, domestic troubles and separation from wife or

children, low companions, loss of wealth and poverty.

With Venus. Unfortunate, low companions, bad environment.

With Mars. Evil companions, bad habits, sex troubles, and afflictions of a Mars-Venus type.

With Jupiter. Hypocrisy, dissipation, business losses and disgrace.

With Saturn. Uncontrolled passions, drink, debauchery, perverted genius, clever writer of undesirable literature, luxurious surroundings but little wealth, isolated or confined at end of life, domestic unhappiness, accidents if Mars is also afflicting.

With Uranus. Legal difficulties, trouble through occultism, danger of imprisonment but help from friends, unfavourable for love and marriage, parental disharmony, little wealth, death from an accident.

With Neptune. Accidents, secret enemies, great psychic powers, wife may be sickly or die soon after marriage, favourable for gain but many losses in latter part of life, sudden troubles of a Mars nature.

16. ALHENA. γ *Geminorum.* ♋ 7° 59'.

Notes. A brilliant white star in the left foot of the Southern Twin, often called Bright Foot of Gemini. From Al Han'ah, a Brand or Mark burnt in. According to Bullinger it means "hurt, wounded or afflicted," and it has been called "the wound in the tendon Achilles.'"

Influence. According to Ptolemy it is of the nature

of Mercury and Venus, but Alvidas gives Moon and Venus. It bestows eminence in art but gives liability to accidents affecting the feet.

With Sun. Pride, love of ease, luxury and pleasure. There may be martial honours but danger of losing them.

With Moon. Good health, honour, riches, pleasure and society, domestic benefits.

With Mercury. Popularity, benefits from opposite sex, musical and artistic ability but little fame, domestic harmony, business adversely affected by pleasure and society.

With Venus. Material concerns, love of dress, pleasure and flattery, artistic and musical ability.

With Mars. Superficial nature, fond of pleasure, ease, luxury, ornament and display.

With Jupiter. Social advancement and success, philosophical mind, love of ostentation.

With Saturn. Caution, reserve, studiousness, prominence in science or art, some domestic discord, sickness to the children, unexpected losses but possibility of wealth, ill-health at the end of life.

With Uranus. Timid, suspicious, selfish, economical over small things and extravagant in large ones, emotional, vacillating, unpractical and much influenced by habits, easily hypnotized, occult interests and secret psychic ability; afflicted with Cancerian ailments; two or more marriages, one very early and extremely unhappy especially if female; unfavourable for home and children. If a woman, good-looking and many friends but enemies among women.

With Neptune. Easily influenced, suffers through indiscreet actions, mediumistic, very sympathetic, often domestic disharmony, unfavourable for gain, death brought about by own acts.

17. AL JABHAH. *η Leonis.* ♌ 26° 47'.
Notes. From Al Jeb'ha, the Forehead. It is situated on the Lion's mane.
Influence. Of the nature of Saturn and Mercury. It gives loss and many dangers, a violent and intemperate nature, and to a military officer danger of mutiny and murder by his soldiers. These characteristics are most marked when the star is rising.

18. ALMACH. *γ Andromedæ.* ♉ 13° 7'.
Notes. A binary (or ternary) star, orange, emerald and blue, situated on the left foot of Andromeda. From Al Anak al Ard, a small Arabian animal like a badger.
Influence. Of the nature of Venus. It gives honour, eminence and artistic ability.

19. ALNILAM. *ε Orionis.* ♊ 22° 22'.
Notes. A bright white star occupying the central position in Orion's Belt. From Al Nitham, the String of Pearls.
Influence. According to Ptolemy it is of the nature of Jupiter and Saturn ; and to Alvidas of Mercury and Saturn. It gives fleeting public honours.
With Sun. Rash, headstrong, surly. If also culminating, military preferment and gain.

With Moon. Many sudden and unexpected losses and reverses, much help from friends, ill-health of family.

With Mercury. Hasty, quick temper, quarrels with associates, domestic disharmony through own actions, troubles through writings and opposite sex.

With Venus. Trouble through love affairs, scandal, enemies among women.

With Mars. Quarrels, loss by lawsuits, domestic disharmony, bad health, violent death.

With Jupiter. Legal or Church preferment but danger of disgrace, loss by speculation, trouble through relatives and foreign affairs.

With Saturn. Courageous, domestic disharmony, leaves home early, successful but many unexpected losses, favourable for health.

With Uranus. Scientific ability, critical, enthusiastic, too many interests, may practise medicine or invent new surgical appliances but reaps no gain from them, many troubles and annoyances, disharmony with brothers and sisters who may cheat native out of inheritance, loss through law and in business, several marriages, enmity between native and partner's relatives, unfavourable for children, sudden death in middle age while travelling, leaving affairs involved in litigation.

With Neptune. Honest, outspoken, hasty in speech, rash and impulsive, offends others through irreligious speech, business and mercantile pursuits or engaged in science, may be head of learned institution or connected with large companies, fond of speculation, sports and the water, quick and level-headed in emergencies, many friends but loss through some, danger of accidents, domestic harmony, dies before old age. (*See* CINGULA ORIONIS.)

20. ALPHARD. α *Hydræ*. ♌ 26° 10'.

Notes. An orange star in the neck of the Hydra From Al Fard al Shuja, the Solitary One in the Serpent. Often called the Hydra's Heart or Cor Hydræ.

Influence. Ptolemy states that it is of the nature of Saturn and Venus, but according to Alvidas it is similar to the Sun and Jupiter in sextile. It gives wisdom, musical and artistic appreciation, knowledge of human nature, strong passions, lack of self-control, immorality, revolting deeds and a sudden death by drowning, poison or asphyxiation.

If rising, much trouble, anxiety and loss in connection with estates and building; addicted to women and intemperance.

With Sun. Power and authority but suffering through own acts and from enemies, loss of position and honour, overcome by enemies.

With Moon. Lust, wantonness, profligacy, failure in projects but financial help often from a relative, ill-fortune to wife or mother, eventual disgrace and ruin, danger of death by asphyxiation. If afflicted by Mars or Saturn, death by drowning or poison especially if Mars be angular. If a malefic is in conjunction with Algol, death by water or poison.

With Mercury. Trouble through writings, unfavourable for marriage, suffering through a passionate attachment that entirely changes the course of the life.

With Venus. Passionate attachments that are

opposed by relatives, handsome and admired by opposite sex, favourable for gain, sorrow through love affairs if female.

With Mars. Trouble and scandal through love affairs. Attachment to a married person. Bad for childbirth, if a woman liable to miscarriage and death, together with death of child, danger of serious accidents; if afflicting luminaries, danger of death by drowning or poison.

With Jupiter. Strong passions, favourable for gain, attachment to widow or widower. liable to disgrace, legal trouble and judicial sentence.

With Saturn. Strong passions but cool, cautious and slow to anger, secret and sorrowful love affairs of short duration, unfavourable for gain, domestic disharmony, danger of death by poison.

With Uranus. Disgrace especially through love affairs, evil habits, unbalanced mind, tendency to great crime, bad for gain and marriage, downfall through love disappointment; if a woman, early ruin and depraved life.

With Neptune. Strong passions, shallow affections, seducer, led astray early in life, bad for gain and marriage, separation from or loss of parents, accidents, public death through secret enemies. If culminating, death of mother at native's birth.

21. ALPHECCA. *a Coronæ Borealis.* ♏ 11° 10'.
Notes. A brilliant white star in the knot of the ribbon. From Al Na'ir al Fakkah, the Bright One of the Dish.

Influence. According to Ptolemy it is of the nature of Venus and Mercury, but Alvidas considers it to be like Mars and Mercury. It gives honour, dignity and poetical and artistic ability.

With Sun. Active and brilliant mind, self-seeking, subject to scandal that does not affect the position.

With Moon. Public honour and dignity, suffers through law, partners and neighbours, trouble through underhanded dealings of enemies but eventual triumph over them, bad for love affairs, some faithful friends, greatly esteemed by Venus and Mercury people.

With Mercury. Mind more active than body, somewhat indolent, benefits from friends, extravagant but saving in small things, loss by enemies.

With Venus. Favourable for love affairs, benefits from friends, artistic and musical tastes.

With Mars. Active mind, better writer than speaker, unfavourable for gain.

With Jupiter. Honour and dignity, artistic ability, benefit through ecclesiastical matters, favourable for material gain.

With Saturn. Studious, popular, economical but poor, benefits from elderly friends, strong but well-controlled passions, poor health, love disappointment but marries above own station, few children but harmonious ties with them.

With Uranus. Selfish, mental affliction and violence at end of life, psychic power, suffering through occultism, deceptive, many false friends, small inheritance obtained with difficulty, losses by law, enemies and mercurial affairs, sorrow through children or an adopted child, domestic trouble through own acts, danger of a violent death.

With Neptune. Aggressive, abrupt, disagreeable,

unfavourable for money matters but gain through marriage, domestic disharmony and peculiar features in connection with marriage, not very favourable for children, gain through martial occupations, may invent something of value in surgery or chemistry, writes on occult subjects, many changes, much travel by water in early life, many enemies, liable to heart ailments, sudden or violent death.

22. ALPHERATZ. α *Andromedæ*. ♈ 13° 11′.

Notes. A double star, white and purplish, in the hair of Andromeda. From Al Surrat al Faras, The Horse's Navel, as it was formerly located in Pegasus. According to Bullinger, though with less likelihood, it is from Al Phiratz, the Broken Down. Frequently called Caput Andromedæ or Andromeda's Head.

Influence. According to Ptolemy it is of the nature of Jupiter and Venus, and to these Alvidas adds Mars also. It gives independence, freedom, love, riches, honour and a keen intellect.

With Sun. Honour, preferment and favours from others.

With Moon. Energetic, persevering, honour, wealth, many good friends and business success.

With Mercury. Active mind, benefits from judges, lawyers or churchmen, pioneer work bringing prominence, accused of selfish motives, writes on science, religion or philosophy.

With Venus. Neat and tidy appearance, quiet life, good health, fond of pleasure and society, fortunate in speculation.

With Mars. Sharp mind, energetic, business success through own endeavours.

With Jupiter. Philosophical or religious mind, benefits from professional men, ecclesiastical honour and dignity, favourable for gain.

With Saturn. Open and affable but miserly, seeks popularity, pretends to be religious for business ends, favours from clergy and lawyers, likelihood of wealth, domestic harmony, liable to diseases in the head and tumours that finally cause death.

With Uranus. Just, honourable, good speaker, domestic harmony if male, but not so fortunate for female, benefit from practical application of ideas, interest in occultism, considerable psychic power if female, favourable for gain.

With Neptune. Sincere, earnest, humane, good speaker and writer, engaged in charitable work, religious reform or animal protection, knowledge of human nature, money sought and obtained chiefly for charitable purposes, many friends, domestic harmony, not very favourable for children.

With a malefic and the Moon at the same time with Sirius, death by a fiery cutting weapon or from beasts; if the Moon be with Wega; violent death.

23. AL PHERG. η *Piscium.* ♈ 25° 42'.

Notes. A double star in the cord near the tail of the Northern Fish. Associated with the Greek Head of Typhon.

Influence. Of the nature of Saturn and Jupiter. It gives preparedness, steadiness, determination and final success.

24. ALTAIR. α *Aquilæ.* ♒ 0° 39′

Notes. A pale yellow star in the neck of the Eagle. From Al Tair, the Eagle, or, according to Bullinger, the Wounding. Sometimes called "The Bird of Jove."

Influence. Opinions are divided as to the exact nature of this star. Ptolemy gives Mars and Jupiter, Wilson, Saturn and Mercury; Simmonite, Uranus; and Alvidas, Uranus and Mercury in sextile to the Sun. It confers a bold, confident, valiant, unyielding, ambitious and liberal nature, great and sudden but ephemeral wealth, and a position of command, makes its natives guilty of bloodshed, and gives danger from reptiles.

With Sun. Public honour, notoriety, favours from superiors, many friends and some envious ones who cause trouble through writings, some ill-health and losses, danger of bites from venomous animals.

With Moon. Interest in a strange or ancient discovery, disappointment and loss over property and gain, some profit and preferment, friends become enemies, trouble through companies or public affairs, difficulties through or misfortune to children.

With Mercury. Many difficulties, misfortunes, and strange experiences. Disappointment on long journeys, bad for partnership, loss of a relative under strange circumstances.

With Venus. Unfavourable for love affairs. Strange and peculiar attractions. Bad for children and gain, losses through friends.

With Mars. Sharp mind, trouble through friends, society and companies but eventual gain.

With Jupiter. Real or pretended religious zeal

hypocrisy, trouble through legal and church matters, and with relatives, bad for gain, disappointment over inheritance.

With Saturn. Sorrow and disappointment, mental disturbance necessitating asylum or hospital treatment and probably death there, separation from family or parents, danger of accident involving inability to work or lifelong affliction.

With Uranus. Cautious, spiritual, sensitive, sympathetic though sometimes abrupt, just, idealistic, interested in occultism but sceptical in religion, reverence for early memories, disappointments throughout life, good mind, considerable gain, faithful literary friends of a Gemini type, some domestic affliction, natural death at a very advanced age.

With Neptune. Over-sensitive, distasteful environment, high ideals, mystic, drifts without personal effort, secret enemies and trouble through occultism, domestic disharmony, sudden and unexpected death.

25. ANTARES. *a Scorpii.* ♐ 8° 39'.

Notes. A binary star, fiery red and emerald green, situated on the body of the Scorpion. From Anti Ares, similar to, or the Rival of Mars. It was one of the four Royal stars of Persia in 3000 B.C., when as the Watcher of the West it marked the Autumnal Equinox. Sometimes called Shiloh and Cor Scorpio, the Scorpion's Heart.

Influence. According to Ptolemy it is of the nature of Mars and Jupiter. Alvidas gives Jupiter sextile Venus, but this is unlikely considering the decidedly martial and malefic nature of the star. It causes malevolence, destructiveness, liberality, broad-mindedness, evil presages and danger of fatality, and makes its natives rash, ravenous, headstrong and destructive to themelves by their own obstinacy.

If rising. Riches and honour, violence, sickness, benefits seldom last.

If culminating. Honour, preferment and good fortune.

With Sun. Pretended religion, insincere, honour and riches ending in disgrace and ruin, military preferment, danger of treachery, violence committed or suffered, fevers and sickness, injuries to the right eye, violent death. If rising or culminating, great honour through violence attended by difficulties and casualties. If with Mars also, pestilential disease.

With Moon. Popular, broad-minded, interested in philosophy, science and metaphysics, liable to change religious opinions, influential friends, favourable for business and domestic matters, active in local affairs, great power, honour and wealth but benefits may not prove lasting, danger of violence, sickness, drowning or assassination. If in 1st or 10th houses, honour and preferment but many dangers and calamities. Liable to blindness or eye injuries especially if at the same time Mars or Saturn be with Regulus. If Saturn be with Aldebaran, danger of a violent death probably by hanging ; but if Mars be with Aldebaran death by a stab, blow or fall especially if in angles. If a malefic be with Aldebaran in the 4th, 7th, 11th or 12th houses, death by a sudden sword-thrust, stab or fall.

With Mercury. Suspicious, wrongfully accuses friends, unpopular, uses ecclesiastical influence in business, money obtained slowly and with much difficulty, danger of sickness to the native and his family, and death of a relative at home or away.

With Venus. Insincere, dishonest, energetic and able but selfish, unfavourable for gain and health.

With Mars. Detrimental habits powerfully affecting the life, quarrels with friends and relatives, fairly favourable for gain. If at the same time the Moon is with Aldebaran, danger of death by sword or hanging.

With Jupiter. Great religious zeal real or pretended, ecclesiastical preferment, tendency to hypocrisy, benefits through relatives.

With Saturn. Materialistic, dishonest through circumstances created by environment, religious hypocrisy, many disappointments, loss through quarrels and legal affairs, trouble through enemies, many failures, hampered by relatives, unfavourable for domestic matters, much sickness to and sorrow from children, If at the same time the Moon is with Aldebaran, danger of death by sword or hanging.

With Uranus. Abnormal and extreme ideas, hypocritical, lies and exaggerates, extremely socialistic, incites to riot, lawlessness and anarchism and in danger of imprisonment on this account, occasional poverty, disharmony with relatives, more than one marriage, unfavourable for children, violent death.

With Neptune. Shrewd, cunning, unbalanced and mentally unsound, secretive but apparently candid, dishonest, tendency to theft, economical, untruthful, strange religious ideas, evil environment, gain through hard work, sudden and unexpected death brought about by treachery or through enemies who will escape retribution.

With Fortuna, or its dispositor, poverty.

26. ARCTURUS. *a Boötis.* ♎ 23° 7'.

Notes. A golden-yellow star situated on the left knee of Boötes. From Arktouros, the Bear Guard. Also called Arctophilax, the Bear Watcher; and Alchameth, Azimech, and other variants of Al Simak, the Lofty One. According to Bullinger Arcturus means He Cometh, and was called Smat, One who rules, and Bau, the Coming One, by the Egyptians.

Influence. According to Ptolemy it is of the nature of Mars and Jupiter, but Alvidas substitutes Venus and Mercury conjoined. It gives riches, honours, high renown, self-determination and prosperity by navigation and voyages.

If rising. Good fortune, with many cares and anxieties through own folly.

If culminating. High office under Government, great profit and reputation. If at the same time with Sun, Moon or Jupiter, ample fortune and great honour.

With Sun. Success through slow and patient plodding, friends among clergy, favourable for gain and for dealing with the public and lawyers.

With Moon. New friends, business success, good judgment, domestic harmony. If with Mars also, danger of death by suffocation.

With Mercury. Sober, industrious, popular, inclined to be religious, somewhat extravagant but well-off, help through friends, holds position of trust in large company or corporation, or receives promotion under direction, favourable for health and domestic affairs.

With Venus. Popular, gifts and favours from friends, some false friends of own sex.

With Mars. Popular, many friends, considerable gain but does not save owing to extravagance. If in 1st, 7th, 9th, 10th or 11th houses and the Moon is at the same time with Pollux, danger of death by suffocation.

With Jupiter. Benefits from legal and Church matters, influential position, danger of hypocrisy gain through foreign affairs or shipping.

With Saturn. Honest, selfish, inclined to be mean, shrewd in business, materialistic, favourable for gain and speculation and for domestic matters, but early difficulty in married life, favourable for children but disagreement with one of them.

With Uranus. Favourable for work entailing quick buying and selling and for dealing with the public, associated with antiques or ancient matters and given to forming collections, associated with art science or literature, official position in some club or society, favourable for gain, benefits from friends, favourable for marriage and children and benefit through both, natural death abroad.

With Neptune. Ingenious, business instincts, changeable, and loss through this means, mediumistic and rather negative, associated with societies as an official, loss and misfortune in middle age which hastens death, favourable for friendship, partnership, marriage and success, greatly dependent upon advice of marriage partner.

27. ARMUS. η *Capricorni.* ≈ 11° 37'.
Notes. Situated in the heart of the Goat.
Influence. Of the nature of Mars and Mercury. It gives disagreeableness, contemptibleness, instability, shamelessness, nagging and a troublesome and contentious nature.

28. ASCELLA. ζ *Sagittarii.* ♑ 12° 31'.
Notes. A binary star situated in the armpit of Sagittarius.
Influence. Of the nature of Jupiter and Mercury. It gives good fortune and happiness.
With Sun. Good fortune and lasting happiness.
With Moon. New and influential friends, valuable gifts, love of respectable women.

29. ASELLI. γ and δ *Cancri.* ♌ 6° 25' and 7° 36'.
Legend. The Aselli represent the asses ridden by Bacchus and Vulcan in the war between the Gods and Titans. The braying of these animals so frightened the latter that they fled, and the Gods in gratitude translated both the asses and their manger (PRÆSÆPE) into heaven.
Notes. Two straw-coloured stars known as the North Asellus (γ) and the South Asellus (δ) from the Latin asellus, a little ass, situated in the body of the Crab.
Influence. According to Ptolemy both the Aselli are of the nature of Mars and the Sun, but Alvidas

states that the North Asellus is like the Sun and Mars in sextile, and the South Asellus like the Sun and Mars in semisquare. Together they give care and responsibility, with a charitable and fostering nature, but danger of violent death, serious accidents and burns. The joint influence of the two Aselli is as follows :

If rising. Burning fevers, bad eyes, blindness of left eye, injuries by beasts, quarrels, slander from low women or vulgar persons, martial preferment.

If culminating. Disgrace and ruin, often violent death

With Sun. Blows, stabs, serious accidents, shooting, shipwreck, beheading, hanging, murderer or murdered, violent fevers, danger of fire, disgrace and imprisonment.

With Moon. Inflammatory fever, pains in the head, blindness.

The separate influences are as follows .

(a) *North Asellus.*

Identified with Balaam's ass. It gives patience, beneficence and courage, and makes its natives heroic and defiant leaders.

With Sun. Favourable for dealing with the public and influential people, business success.

With Moon. Favourable for material success, honour through public positions, help from friends, favourable for gain, danger of accidents to the head, fevers, inflammatory ailments, and heart weakness.

With Mercury. Power and authority after many difficulties, little gain, numerous expenses, losses by writings, mortgages and bonds.

With Venus. Proud, opinionated, help from an influential friend, favourable for gain.

With Mars. Courageous, generous, noble, just, power and authority.

With Jupiter. Great gain and influential position, favours from churchmen and gain through legal and ecclesiastical matters, benefits from foreign affairs.

With Saturn. Somewhat self-centred and self-seeking, loss through enemies, high public office, but eventual retirement with public censure. Favourable for gain, unrelenting nature, domestic disharmony caused by antipathy between one of the children and the native or partner.

With Uranus. Energetic, reformer, blunt in speech and often bitter, fixed ideas, honest, careless or broad in religion, many friends among the public, some of whom abuse confidence, enemies among the higher classes, governmental position, involved in disputes with corporations owing to socialistic interests, favourable for gain and domestic matters, likelihood of unexpected death abroad.

With Neptune. Proud, haughty, great self-esteem, occult interests, prominent and influential position in a company concerned with stocks and shares or speculation, connected with schools or places of amusement, early difficulties with parents, favourable for gain but danger of loss by fire or theft, favourable for marriage but sometimes one of convenience. With Mars also, accidents and danger of fatal injuries.

(b) *South Asellus.*

Called the Mare Ass, A Resting Place, and the Ending or Stop.

With Sun. Unfavourable for dealing with the public and influential people, trouble in business.

With Moon. Ill-health, defective sight, hearing or speech; bad for business affairs, loss of friends and trouble through enemies.

With Mercury. Mental affliction, much worry and disappointment, loss by fire of valuable papers, bad for success in spite of help from friends, difficulties brought about by children.

With Venus. Trouble through friends, unfavourable for love and marriage, enmity of women, too fond of pleasure and society.

With Mars. Energy, courage, misapplied powers, little success, public disfavour.

With Jupiter. Legal and ecclesiastical troubles, hypocrisy, dishonesty, false friends, danger of imprisonment.

With Saturn. Untrustworthy, dishonourable, low morality, bad habits formed early in life.

With Uranus. Seeks applause, suffers from own mistakes, seldom sees own faults, official positions of short duration, downfall brought about by enemies, self-seeking, loss or ruin through speculation, bad for gain and domestic matters, danger of accident causing lingering death.

With Neptune. Ambitious but indolent; if male, handsome, pleasant and affable and a lady's man; if female, rather masculine in appearance and character; many love affairs causing general suffering, losses through speculation, unmerited favours from friends, advantageous marriage but domestic disharmony, fevers and violent diseases, sometimes causing death in infancy.

30. BATEN KAITOS. ʒ *Ceti.* ♈ 20° 50′.

Notes. A topaz-yellow star in the body of the Whale. From Al Batn al Kaitos, the Whale's Belly.

Influence. Of the nature of Saturn. It gives compulsory transportation, change or emigration, misfortune by force or accident, shipwreck but also rescue, falls and blows.

31. BELLATRIX. γ *Orionis.* ♊ 19° 50′.

Notes. A slightly variable pale-yellow star on the left shoulder of Orion. The name means the Female Warrior, but according to Bullinger it signifies Quickly Coming or Swiftly Destroying.

Influence. According to Ptolemy it is like Mars and Mercury; and, to Alvidas, Mercury and Mars in good aspect. It gives great civil or military honour but danger of sudden dishonour, renown, wealth, eminent friends and liability to accidents causing blindness and ruin. If prominent in a woman's map it makes her loquacious and shrewish, and gives a high-pitched, hard and sharp voice.

If culminating. Quarrels, hatred, fraud committed or suffered, forgery, swindling, coining and perjury.

With Sun. Vacillating, changeable, indecisive in business, mechanical ability, riches and honour but final ruin, blindness by accident, disease, extreme sickness, fevers or violent death.

With Moon. Luxury, lust, vain ambition, waste, ruin, blindness by accidents, great power, honour and wealth, honour in martial matters, as soldier, surgeon, metal worker; may attain distinction through courage.

With Mercury. Honour and preferment in military matters, favourable for friendship and social affairs.

With Venus. Much suffering through love affairs owing to unrestrained feelings.

With Mars. Strength, energy, success as soldier, surgeon or metal worker, liable to accidents.

With Jupiter. Philosophical and religious mind, hypocrisy, may be fanatic, legal prominence, and great honour but danger of slander.

With Saturn. Secluded and studious life, reserved, thoughtful, unfavourable for gain owing to lack of interest, poverty at end of life, often single but if married the partner may die young, no children.

With Uranus. Mental disturbance, much activity, occult or unpractical interests, repeatedly suffers through the same mistakes, disharmony with relatives and neighbours, successful in the occupation of making peculiar machinery but little financial gain ; unfavourable for domestic matters, many minor accidents.

With Neptune. Keen intellect, extremist, little forethought or balance, many quarrels, ability for mercantile pursuits, associated with companies connected with patents or electrical instruments, bad for marriage or partnership, many unexpected events, fairly good for gain, many narrow escapes but eventual violent death.

32. BETELGEUZE. α *Orionis.* ♊ 27° 38'.

Notes. An irregularly variable orange star situated on the right shoulder of Orion. From Ibt al Jauzah, the Armpit of the Central One or Giant, but meaning according to Bullinger the Coming of the Branch.

Influence. According to Ptolemy it is of the nature of Mars and Mercury ; and, to Alvidas, of Mercury, Saturn and Jupiter in good aspect. It gives martial honour, preferment and wealth.

If culminating. Great military fortune, command, invention, ingenuity and helps in the perfection of arts and sciences. If at the same time with Sun, Moon or Jupiter, ample fortune and great honour.

With Sun. Interest in and ability for occult and mystical subjects; acute diseases, fevers, honour and preferment ending in final ruin.

With Moon. Active mind, strong will, turbulent, rebellious under restraint, military success but suffering through quarrels with superiors, likelihood of great power, honour and wealth.

With Mercury. Serious, studious, scientific and literary ; unfavourable for gain, fame through writings or engravings in metal, favourable for health but liable to accidents.

With Venus. Somewhat retiring and reserved, great ability as a maker of fine ornaments, favourable for gain, some sorrow connected with the family or marriage.

With Mars. Cautious, reserved, good leader and organizer, honour and preferment in martial matters.

With Jupiter. Serious and studious mind, shrewd and profitable business dealings, great honour in the Church or law.

With Saturn. Shrewd, cunning, craftily dishonest, treacherous to friends, eventful life with many ups and downs, eventual wealth but little comfort, unfavourable for domestic matters.

With Uranus. Quick, active and evil mind, clever criminal, notorious as forger or counterfeiter but rarely caught, quiet pleasant manner, generous and not bad at heart, possesses hypnotic and thought-reading powers.

With Neptune. Ingenious, mechanical ability, may invent mechanical device, spiritualistic interests, some physical ailment or affliction or mental derangement, not good for gain but greatest success in partnership, favourable for marriage and children but disharmony with brothers and sisters, liable to some serious or fatal accident in middle age.

33. BOS. ρ *Capricorni.* ♒ 4° 3'.

Notes. A small star situated in the Goat's face.

Influence. Of the nature of Saturn and Venus. It gives a clever and piercing intellect if in conjunction with Mercury.

34. BUNGULA. α *Centauri.* ♏ 28° 28'.

Notes. A binary star, white and yellowish, on the left forefoot of the Centaur. According to Bullinger it bore the ancient name Toliman, meaning the Heretofore and Hereafter. It is the nearest to our system of all the stars and lies at a distance of about 275,000 times that of the earth from the Sun.

Influence. According to Ptolemy it is of the nature of Venus and Jupiter; and, to Alvidas, of Mars with the Moon and Uranus in Scorpio. It gives beneficence, friends, refinement and a position of honour.

With Sun. Envious, self-centred, slow but fairly successful progress, many enemies, loss of inheritance.

With Moon. Popular, many friends, diplomatic, secret bad habits, excessive drinking, involved in disputes but emerges successfully.

With Mercury. Changeable, vacillating, fault-finding, difficult to please, good intellect, business success, trouble in domestic affairs through enemies, family sickness, disappointed ambitions.

With Venus. Popular, artistic and musical abilities, benefits from friends, danger from love affairs.

With Mars. Physical endurance, considerable mental power, speaker or writer, little prominence.

With Jupiter. Great ecclesiastical or legal honour and preferment, ritualistic tendencies, success in foreign countries, favourable for gain.

With Saturn. Studious, well read, materialistic, self-seeking, favourable for gain, accumulation of money and property and legacies, though not without quarrels, favourable for marriage though some domestic disturbance, eldest child may be afflicted in early life.

With Uranus. Selfish, self-seeking, jealous of others' success, dishonest, determined but indecisive in some things, loss through law, enemies and mercurial affairs, little prominence at home and greater reputation abroad, loss of friends, death through virulent disease.

With Neptune. Occult interests, psychic or mediumistic, deceitful, dishonest, many journeys and voyages often to the east of birthplace, rarely long in one place, occupation of a watery nature or connected with places of amusement and small speculations, favourable for gain and domestic matters, heavy business losses at end of life, death caused by Scorpio ailment.

35. CANOPUS. α *Argus*. ♋ 13° 51'.

Notes. A white star in one of the oars of the ship Argo. Named in honour of Canopus, the chief pilot of the fleet of Menelaus, who was killed in Egypt by the bite of a serpent on his return from the destruction of Troy.

Influence. According to Ptolemy it is of the nature of Saturn and Jupiter; and, to Alvidas, of the Moon and Mars. It gives piety, conservatism, a wide and comprehensive knowledge, voyages and educational work, and changes evil to good.

If culminating. Great glory, fame and wealth, dignity and authority by the help of an old clergyman or influential person.

With Sun. Domestic affliction, trouble with father or parents, financial loss, danger of accidents, burns and fevers, unfavourable end to life.

With Moon. Success in martial matters as a soldier, surgeon, metal worker, etc.

With Mercury. Rash, headstrong, stubborn, kind-hearted, speaker or writer on unpopular subjects incurring criticism; trouble and loss through domestic matters, partners and law.

With Venus. Emotional, sensitive, stubborn, strong passions, scandal through an intrigue by which reputation will suffer, public disgrace, bad for gain.

With Mars. Cruel, bad-tempered, envious, jealous.

With Jupiter. Great pride, religion used for business ends, voyages, honour and preferment but reversal through public dissatisfaction.

With Saturn. Discontented, occult interests, unfavourable for reputation and domestic matters, little prominence but may do good.

With Uranus. Materialistic, dishonourable, many difficulties, easily influenced, estranged from relatives and friends, trouble through enemies and opposite sex, domestic disharmony, violent and possibly public death.

With Neptune. Aggressive, materialistic, strong mind and body, loss through quarrels, speculation and friends, ideas or inventions often stolen, peculiar events throughout life, unexpected losses and gains, disharmony with father in earlier life, liable to accidents, sudden death.

36. CAPELLA. α *Aurigæ.* ♊ 20° 44'.

Notes. A white star situated on the body of the Goat in the arms of Auriga. The name means Little She-Goat. Sometimes called Amalthea in honour of the nurse who reared Jupiter upon the milk of the goat.

Influence. According to Ptolemy it is of the nature of Mars and Mercury ; and, to Alvidas, of Mercury and the Moon. It gives honour, wealth, eminence, renown, a public position of trust and eminent friends, and makes its natives careful, timorous, inquisitive, very fond of knowledge and particularly of novelties.

If culminating. Military, naval or ecclesiastical connections and preferment, waste, dissipation, envy and trouble. If at the same time with Sun, Moon or Jupiter, ample fortune and great honour.

With Sun. Vacillating, changeable, too loquacious, quick speech, misunderstood and criticized, martial honour and wealth.

With Moon. Inquisitive, loquacious, indiscreet speech, sarcastic, quarrelsome, many journeys and voyages, domestic disharmony, danger to sight, liable to accidents.

With Mercury. Disagreeable experiences, legal action over writings and success after much difficulty.

With Venus. Literary and poetical ability, unfavourable for gain.

With Mars. Intellectual, learned, talents wasted on low subjects.

With Jupiter. Legal or ecclesiastical connections, slander and criticism, too enthusiastic or zealous, many voyages, trouble with relatives.

With Saturn. Shrewd, tidy, fond of luxury, many detrimental habits, makes much money but does not keep it, trouble from opposite sex and domestic disharmony, bad health at end of life and afflicted in arms, legs or eyes necessitating restricted movement.

With Uranus. Eccentric, mentally unbalanced or insane, clever inventor especially in connection with electricity, dependent upon others, little gain, peculiar religious views, unfavourable for domestic affairs; children, if any, weak in intellect.

With Neptune. Prominent psychological writer, high ambitions and moderate success, courageous, rash, studious, connected with inventions to do with methods of transit, many journeys, peculiar hygienic ideas, disharmony with brothers, unfavourable for children, accidents in early life, health collapses in middle age necessitating confinement but mental faculties remain active.

37. CAPHIR. γ *Virginis.* ♎ 9° 2'.

Notes. A binary and slightly variable white star on the left arm of Virgo. Called An Atonement Offering and the Submissive One.

Influence. According to Ptolemy it is of the nature of Mercury and Venus ; to Simmonite, of Mercury alone ; and, to Alvidas, of Venus and Mars. It gives a courteous, refined and lovable character with prophetic instincts.

With Sun. Involved in an intrigue. some difficulty of short duration leaving native in unpleasant position.

With Moon. Popular, business worries, domestic disharmony and divorce, poor health.

With Mercury. Legal troubles, criticism, many worries, business difficulties which will be overcome, ill-health, loses respect of associates.

With Venus. Unfavourable for gain, much scandal from passionate love affair.

With Mars. Loss through lawsuits and by fire or storm, trouble with opposite sex, marriage partner and public.

With Jupiter. Trouble through legal affairs or with the Church, disputes over inheritance, domestic disharmony through intrigue and consequent scandal.

With Saturn. Intelligent, studious, home troubles in early life, evil environment, liable to imprisonment or execution for another's crime especially if in 12th house, suffers through conspiracy of friends or relatives, domestic disharmony, sickly children, home broken up, death in prison.

With Uranus. Well-educated, good intellect, easily influenced, led astray into extremely unpleasant environment by false friends, strong passions, often remains single, frequent accidents to the head, sudden and unexpected death through accident.

With Neptune. Shrewd and cunning for evil, changes in early life, many disappointments affecting the mental balance, abnormal religious enthusiasm, unpractical and useless pursuits, bad for gain, marriage and children.

38. Capulus. 33 ♑ vi *Persei*. ♉ 23° 5′.

Notes. A double cluster situated in the sword hand of Perseus.

Influence. Of the nature of Mars and Mercury. It causes blindness or defective eyesight.

39. Castor. α *Geminorum*. ♋ 19° 8′.

Notes. A binary star, bright white and pale white, situated on the head of the Northern Twin. It represents Castor, the mortal one of the twins, famous for his skill in taming and managing horses. Sometimes called Apollo, and symbolically named A Ruler yet to Come.

Influence. According to Ptolemy it is of the nature of Mercury; to Wilson, Simmonite and Pearce, of Mars, Venus and Saturn; and, to Alvidas, of the Moon, Mars and Uranus. It gives distinction, a keen intellect, success in law and publishing, many travels, fondness for horses, sudden fame and honour but often followed by loss of fortune and disgrace, sickness, trouble and great affliction. Its natives are said to be mischievous and prone to violence.

If rising. Blindness, bad eyes, injuries to the face, disgrace, stabs, wounds, imprisonment.

With Sun. Prominence in occult matters, government work dealing with foreign affairs, serious accidents, blows, stabs, shooting, shipwreck, injuries to the face, blindness, disease, violent fevers, evil disposition, rape or murder committed or suffered, imprisonment, banishment, decapitation.

With Moon. Timid, sensitive, lacks confidence, occult interest and psychic ability, blindness, injuries to face, disgrace, stabs, wounds, imprisonment.

With Mercury. Remarkable psychic powers entailing criticism and ridicule but eventual prominence, unfavourable for gain.

With Venus. Strange and peculiar life, many extreme ups and downs, unfavourable for marriage.

With Mars. Evil disposition, much travel, aimless life, many ups and downs.

With Jupiter. Philosophical and occult interests, loss through law, speculation or travel, danger of judicial sentence.

With Saturn. Timid, distrustful, eccentric, original mind but difficulty in expression, better writer than speaker, considerable intellectual powers, fond of detail, prejudiced against popular opinions, unfavourable for marriage, peculiar domestic conditions, early sickness of children, gain at end of life through hard work.

With Uranus. Conscientious, sensitive, impressionable, great psychic power entailing much public criticism, desirous of pleasing all, favourable for marriage and gain, few, if any, children but harmonious relations with them, loss in early life of the parent of opposite sex to native.

With Neptune. Emotional, romantic, fond of pleasure and amusement, connected with or notoriety through watery matters, occult interests, theatrical work and acting, especially in parts where no speaking is required, many removals and journeys, some domestic disharmony or separation, marries too young especially if female, good for gain but loss through friends and speculation, trouble through one or more of the children, death through some Cancer ailment.

40. CASTRA. ε *Capricorni.* ♒ 19° 5′.
Notes. A small star in the Goat's Belly.
Influence. Of the nature of Saturn and Jupiter. It gives malevolence, destructiveness and an uncontrollable temper.

41. CINGULA ORIONIS. δ *and* ε *Orionis.* ♊ 21° 16′
    and 22° 22′. (See MINTAKA and ALNILAM.)
Notes. Orion's Belt, of which the chief stars are Mintaka and Alnilam.
Influence. The separate influences will be found under the above-named stars. The joint influence is to give strength, energy, industry, organizing abilities, notoriety, good fortune, lasting happiness, a sharp mind and a good memory.
If rising. Legacies, love or dissipation, gravity and austerity.

With Sun. Notoriety, good fortune, lasting happiness.

With Moon. Blindness of at least one eye, new and influential friends, valuable gifts, love of respectable women. If a malefic be with Markab, drowning. If the moon is with Saturn also, drowning and assassination.

With a malefic and the Moon at the same time with Markab, death at human hands.

42. COPULA. 51 *M Canum Venaticorum.* ♍ 23° 58'.

Notes. The Spiral or Whirlpool Nebula mentioned by Ptolemy as the nebula under the tail of the Great Bear.

Influence. It is of the nature of the Moon and Venus, and causes blindness, defective eyesight, strong passions, hindrances and disappointments.

43. DABIH. *β Capricorni.* ♒ 2° 56'.

Notes. A double (but telescopically multiple) star, orange yellow and sky blue situated in the left eye of the Goat.

Influence. According to Ptolemy it is of the nature of Saturn and Venus ; and, to Alvidas, of Uranus and Saturn conjoined in square to Mercury.

With Sun. Reserved, suspicious and mistrustful, loss through friends, responsible public position of trust and authority.

With Moon. Successful in business but retires under a cloud, favourable for wealth, influential position but scarcely realizes ambitions, trouble through opposite sex, deserved criticism and censure.

With Mercury. Reserved, suspicious, envious.

self-centred, prominent position in public affairs or companies, favourable for gain, bad for domestic affairs, peculiar home conditions.

With Venus. Secret love affairs, sorrow and disappointment, easily led astray, enmity of women.

With Mars. Great ambition, energy, high position but danger of reversal, domestic disharmony.

With Jupiter. Hypocrisy, dishonesty, high legal or ecclesiastical preferment but ultimate disgrace.

With Saturn. Melancholy, studious, recluse, restless and nervous, writer, accumulates wealth in miserly fashion, often lives alone but if married danger of separation and divorce, wrapt up in some great sorrow, long life.

With Uranus. Strange and peculiar experiences, many ups and downs, much suffering, loses friends through deception, disappointed ambitions, losses of a Mercurial nature, unfavourable for domestic affairs, terror of death, dies after a lingering illness.

With Neptune. Active mind, shrewd and selfish in business, pessimistic, critical, many enemies, occupied with secret undertakings, serious accidents in middle age, disappointing love affairs, unfavourable for early marriage but favourable for one in middle age, prominence in public affairs, sudden death

44. DENEB. ζ *Aquilæ.* ♑ 18° 41′.

Notes. A green star in the Eagle's tail. From Al Dhanab, the Tail.

Influence. Of the nature of Mars and Jupiter. It gives ability to command, liberality, success in war and beneficence.

45. DENEB ADIGE. α *Cygni.* ⣗ 4° 14′.

Notes. A brilliant white star in the tail of the Swan. From Al Dhanab al Dajajah, the Hen's Tail.

Influence. It is of the nature of Venus and Mercury, and gives an ingenious nature and a clever intellect that is quick at learning.

With Sun and Mars above the earth, and the Moon at the same time with Procyon, death by the bite of a mad dog

46. DENEB ALGEDI. δ *Capricorni.* ⣗ 22° 25′.

Notes. A small star in the Goat's tail. From Al Dhanab al Jady, the Tail of the Goat. Symbolically called the Judicial Point of the Goat.

Influence. According to Ptolemy it is of the nature of Saturn and Jupiter ; and, to Alvidas, of Uranus and Mercury in Aquarius in opposition to Saturn in Leo. It is said to cause beneficence and destructiveness, sorrow and happiness, and life and death.

If culminating. Great glory, fame, wealth, dignity and authority by the help of an old clergyman or influential person.

With Sun. Loss through false friends, high position but final disgrace and ruin, loss of money or property, sickness, worry through children.

With Moon. Great difficulties in everything, success after patient plodding but final loss of position.

With Mercury. Melancholy, quiet, solitary, unkempt or ragged, student of nature, science or philosophy, engaged in trapping animals or reptiles, snakes or poisonous beetles which do not harm the native

With Venus. Some secret desire that is never gratified, domestic or family difficulties.

With Mars. Danger from enemies, accidents honour and preferment but many quarrels and final disgrace, violent death.

With Jupiter. Disappointment in secret wishes, false friends, loss through the law, Church and relatives.

With Saturn. Great power over animals and poisonous reptiles, indifferent to study, knowledge of many secrets of nature, feared, unpleasant appearance and life, bad for gain and marriage, death of or separation from parents in youth, secluded end of life.

With Uranus. Many sorrows, engaged in reform, unbalanced mind, may seek someone's life as a mission, unfavourable for gain and marriage, strange and peculiar or violent death.

With Neptune. Easily influenced, psychic ability, superstitious, reserved, economical, some gain through speculation, many enemies, bad early environment leaving lasting impression, morose and melancholy at end of life, accidents, death in a fit or by assassination.

47. DENEBOLA. *β Leonis.* ♍ 20° 30′.

Notes. A blue star in the Lion's tail. From Al Dhanab al Asad, the Tail of the Lion, or, according to Bullinger, the Judge, or Lord who Cometh. Frequently abbreviated to Deneb and so given in most astrological works, but this title properly belongs to another star already described.

Influence. According to Ptolemy it is of the

nature of Saturn and Venus ; to Wilson and Pearce, of Saturn, Venus and Mercury ; to Simmonite, of Uranus ; and, to Alvidas, of Mercury, Uranus and Mars. It gives swift judgment, despair, regrets, public disgrace, misfortune from the elements of nature, and happiness turned to anger, and makes its natives noble, daring, self-controlled, generous and busy with other people's affairs.

If rising. Riches, preferment and good fortune attended by many dangers and anxieties through own folly, benefits seldom last, trouble and sickness.

With Sun. Honour and preferment with danger, public disgrace and final ruin, disease, fevers and acute ailments, death by suicide.

With Moon. Honour and preferment among the vulgar, but final disgrace and ruin, violent disease of vital organ, blindness and injuries to the eyes, accidents, losses through servants, domestic quarrels, temporary separation from marriage partner. If at the same time Saturn or Mars is with Algol, death by sentence.

With Mercury. Many losses through agents or servants and through writings, bad for gain, loss of one of the family through malignant or contagious disease.

With Venus. Strong passions, led astray early in life, ruined through love affairs.

With Mars. Bitter, vindictive, cruel, unpopular, loss of position and public disgrace.

With Jupiter. Pride, hypocrisy, disappointed life, troubles abroad or through relatives, secret enemies, danger of imprisonment or death by sentence.

With Saturn. Critical, always complaining, many enemies, loss through servants and thieves, unfortunate life, domestic sorrow, wife afflicted or children mentally unsound or deformed.

With Uranus. Subject to fits, idiotic, insane, and sometimes violent, sharp and cunning, may commit murder during insanity, confined in asylum, death often by suicide.

With Neptune. Disagreeable, ingenious, clever, sarcastic, bitter in speech, domestic quarrels, accidents and sickness in early life, death in middle age by an accident or lingering illness.

48. DIFDA. β *Ceti.* ♈ 1° 28'.

Notes. A yellow star on the Whale's tail. From Al Difdi al Thani, the Second Frog.

Influence. According to Ptolemy it is of the nature of Saturn ; and, to Alvidas, of Mars, Saturn and Mercury. It causes self-destruction by brute force, sickness, disgrace, misfortune and compulsory change.

With Sun. Mental disturbance, some loss keenly felt, accidents such as burns, scalds and cuts.

With Moon. Pioneer, reckless, headstrong, violent temper, many quarrels, bad for gain and business.

With Mercury. Active mind, writer or speaker upon subjects of public welfare, seeks to enact laws of benefit to the community, favourable for social affairs.

With Venus. Reserved, passionate, many secret love affairs.

With Mars. Passionate, violent, subject to accidents and injuries to the head, fevers, disgrace and ruin through own acts.

With Jupiter. High legal or ecclesiastical position, but danger of reversal, treachery from secret enemies, loss through speculation.

With Saturn. Impure mind, worry, secret wrong-doing, inharmonious environment.

With Uranus. Quick mind, but slow expression, many losses especially in Mercurial matters, restless, much travel, rarely remains long in one place, much energy, but accomplishes little, mind temporarily unbalanced, bad for love affairs and marriage, ailments affecting the kidneys or veins in the small of the back, peculiar death, probably alone in a forest or desert.

With Neptune. Disagreeable, fixed opinions, mechanical and inventive ability, but little gain, peculiar religious ideas, very zealous, domestic disagreements, sorrow caused through some secret, trouble through children, disagreement with or separation from parent, harm through anonymous letters, loss through mercurial affairs and fire, death often by fire.

49. DIRAH. *μ Geminorum.* ♋ 4° 11′.

Notes. A double star, crocus yellow and blue, in the left foot of the Northern Twin. From Al Dirah, the Seed or Branch. Symbolically called the Abused or Beaten One.

Influence. Of the nature of Mercury and Venus. It gives force, energy, power and protection.

50. DORSUM. *θ Capricorni.* ♒ 12° 43′.

Notes. A small star situated on the back of the Goat.

Influence. It is of the nature of Saturn and Jupiter and is of unfortunate influence.

With Sun or Mars. Danger of bites from venomous creatures.

51. EL NATH. β *Tauri.* ♊ 21° 27′.

Notes. A double star, pure brilliant white and pale grey, situated on the tip of the northern horn of the Bull, and commonly known as the Bull's North Horn. From Al Natih, the Butting One, or according to Bullinger the Wounded or Slain. Symbolically called the Shepherd. The name El Nath is often erroneously used for Hamal in Aries.

Influence. Of the nature of Mars and Mercury. It gives fortune, eminence and neutrality for good or evil.

With Sun. Ecclesiastical preferment, honour through science, religion or philosophy.

With Moon. Quarrels with questionable associates, business success, environment detrimental owing to wife, partner or relative.

With Mercury. Favour of superiors, but enmity of colleagues, rises to high position or changes vocation, favourable for gain, but many small losses, domestic expenses, often obliged to support an invalid.

With Venus. Favourable for gain, enemies who are powerless to injure.

With Mars. Good lawyer, speaker, and debater, quick-witted.

With Jupiter. Success in legal or ecclesiastical affairs, favourable for gain and inheritance.

With Saturn. Cautious, thoughtful, bad-tempered, accumulates money, favourable for domestic affairs, gain through relatives, may receive start in life through a legacy.

With Uranus. Great mental energy and force of character, weak body, original and practical ideas, occult interests, but material aims, late success, favourable for domestic affairs, death in middle age.

With Neptune. Active in mind and body, vacillating, some physical defect, occult interests, may make discoveries in medicine, domestic disharmony owing to peculiar matrimonial ideas, may become famous, death in middle age.

52. ENSIS. 42 *M Orionis.* ♊ 21° 55'.
Notes. The Great Nebula in the sword-sheath of Orion.
Influence. Of the nature of Mars and the Moon. It causes blindness, defective sight, injuries to the eyes, sickness and a violent death.

53. FACIES. 22 *M Sagittarii.* ♑ 7° 12'.
Notes. The nebula in the Archer's Face.
Influence. It is of the nature of the Sun and Mars, and causes blindness, defective sight, sickness, accidents and a violent death.

54. FOMALHAUT. α *Piscis Australis.* ♓ 2° 44'.
Notes. A reddish star in the mouth of the Southern Fish. From Fum al Hut, the Fish's Mouth. It was one of the four Royal Stars of Persia in 3000 B.C., when as the Watcher of the South it marked the winter solstice.
Influence. According to Ptolemy, it is of the

nature of Venus and Mercury ; and, to Alvidas, of Jupiter in square to Saturn from Pisces and Sagittarius. It is said to be very fortunate and powerful and yet to cause malevolence of sublime scope and character, and change from a material to a spiritual form of expression. Cardan stated that together with the stars rising with 12 ♊ it gives an immortal name.

If rising or culminating. Great and lasting honours.

With Sun. Dissipated, easily influenced by low companions, gain through inheritance but unproductive of good, may suffer for some crime committed, danger of bites from venomous creatures.

With Moon. Secret business causing much trouble and enmity, but eventual gain after many difficulties. The separation is more benefic than the application.

With Mercury. Many losses and disappointments, unlucky in business, better servant than master, writes or receives secret letters, worry through slander, imprisonment or damaged reputation, domestic difficulties, sickness of a Saturnian nature.

With Venus. Secret and passionate love affairs, some restriction in the life, disappointments, easily led astray.

With Mars. Malevolent, passionate, revengeful, many secret enemies, liable to disgrace and ruin, danger of bites from venomous creatures.

With Jupiter. Sympathetic, charitable, honour in the Church, Freemasonry or secret societies, many voyages.

With Saturn. Accidents, ailments affecting the

lungs, throat and feet, loss through enemies, friends, Mercurial affairs, bands and companies, wrongfully accused, affairs involved at end of life, sudden death and family cheated out of their rights.

With Uranus. Unstable, wasted talents, evil environment, unpractical ideas, loses friends, addicted to drugs or intoxicants, utopian schemes, afflicted marriage partner, brings misfortune to associates, fatally injured by electricity, explosion or accident.

With Neptune. Sharp, shrewd, self-seeking, analytical, detective ability, many secret enemies, connected with secret affairs or government work, occult interests, somewhat dishonest, influential friends, associated with 9th and 12th house affairs, gain through speculation, death of marriage partner, many narrow escapes, violent death through secret enemies.

55. FORAMEN. *η Argus.* ♎ 21° 3'.

Notes. An irregularly variable reddish star situated in the stern of the Ship, and surrounded by the Keyhole nebula.

Influence. Of the nature of Saturn and Jupiter. It causes peril, dignity, piety, usefulness and acquisitiveness, and gives danger to the eyes.

With Sun. Danger of shipwreck.

56. GIEDI. *a Capricorni.* ♒ 2° 42'.

Notes. A multiple star, yellow, ash and lilac. situated on the south horn of the Goat. From Al Jady, the Goat. Symbolically called the Slain Kid.

Influence. According to Ptolemy it is of the

nature of Venus and Mars ; to Simmonite, of Venus and Mercury ; and, to Alvidas, of Uranus in sextile to Venus. It gives beneficence, sacrifice and offering.

With Sun. Peculiar events, unexpected losses and gains, sometimes great good fortune.

With Moon. Peculiar and unexpected events, eccentric, public criticism, new and influential friends, valuable gifts, love of respectable women but difficulties and sometimes platonic marriage.

With Mercury. Romantic, psychic, vacillating, bad for gain, many love affairs some of which cause notoriety, may elope with married person.

With Venus. Many strange and unexpected events, peculiar and romantic marriage, may be separated for years from partner through secret government or political reasons of which even native may be ignorant.

With Mars. Abrupt, aggressive, much criticism, public position.

With Jupiter. Government position, preferment in law or Church, marriage abroad, favourable for gain and inheritance.

With Saturn. Genius but kept down by circumstances, peculiar and occult early environment, birth amidst strange conditions while mother is travelling, many narrow escapes, associated with the stage, rarely marries, unfavourable for gain.

With Uranus. Peculiar environment, bad morals, strong passions, genial, affectionate, vacillating, small self-confidence, too trusting, peculiar ideas on marriage and religion, ambitious but too weak to rise, bad for domestic affairs and children, if any, though there may be illegitimate ones, violent death.

With Neptune. Psychic in childhood, never understood by others, cruelty from a parent, many disappointments, peculiar conditions in domestic life, little success, greatly influenced by others, minor accidents, death in early life or middle age.

57. GRAFFIAS. *β Scorpii.* ♐ 2° 4'.

Notes. A triple star, pale white and lilac, situated on the head of the Scorpion, and frequently called Frons Scorpii.

Influence. According to Ptolemy it is of the nature of Mars and Saturn ; and, to Alvidas, of Jupiter in square to Saturn and the Moon. It causes extreme malevolence, mercilessness, fiendishness, repulsiveness, malice, theft, crime, pestilence, and contagious diseases.

If rising. Riches and preferment attended by danger, violence, trouble, sickness, benefits seldom last.

With Sun. Materialistic, too active a mind, ecclesiastical difficulties, bad health. Otherwise similar to the effect if rising.

With Moon. Great power, honour, wealth, gifts, difficulty in obtaining legacy, materialistic, interested in unpopular ideas, criticized, success after many difficulties. Otherwise similar to the effect if rising.

With Mercury. Dull mind, difficulty in expression or defect in speech, gifts, difficulty in obtaining legacy but final success.

With Venus. Dishonest, self-seeking, energetic, able, favourable for gain.

With Mars. Athletic, suffers from over-exertion.

goes to extremes, active mind, favourable for money matters but extravagant and has many debts.

With Jupiter. Hypocritical, real or pretended religious zeal, legacies attended by legal difficulties.

With Saturn. Cautious, cunning, self-seeking, deceitful, dishonourable, progressive ideas, religious but hypocritical, proud of home, loss by fire or water, gain through marriage and partnership, few children, long life.

With Uranus. Scientific, religious or philosophical work, difficulties with marriage partner's relatives, favourable for marriage and children, domestic difficulties finally overcome, trouble with parents in early life, favourable for gain and speculation, loss through Mercurial matters, liable to accidents by fire and electricity, sudden death.

With Neptune. Connected with science, inventions, companies, or journalism, breeds horses or cattle, good mind, late but favourable marriage but peculiar domestic conditions, accidents in middle age, death after lingering illness.

58. HAMAL. *α Arietis.* ♉ 6° 32′.

Notes. A yellow star situated in the forehead of the Ram and commonly known as the ram's Following Horn. From Al Hamal, the Sheep. Symbolically called the Death Wound and often incorrectly named El Nath.

Influence. According to Ptolemy it is of the nature of Mars and Saturn ; and, to Alvidas, of Venus and Saturn. It causes violence brutishness, cruelty and premeditated crime.

With Sun. Dissipation, evil associates, loss and disgrace.

With Moon. Patient, slow success through hard work, trouble through love affairs but favourable for marriage, marriage partner gains by business or speculation.

With Mercury. Dull mind, many friends, great determination, tactful, greatly influenced by marriage partner.

With Venus. Handsome, quiet, envious, jealous, domestic trouble, ill-health to native or family.

With Mars. Violence, criminal tendencies, influential position but final disgrace and ruin.

With Jupiter. Dissipated, hypocritical, legal or ecclesiastical preferment, loss by speculation.

With Saturn. Cautious, thoughtful, critical, sarcastic, materialistic, interested in geology or agriculture, some domestic happiness, favourable for gain.

With Uranus. Pleasant, sympathetic, easily influenced, sensitive, strong passions, weak nature, mediumistic, drink or detrimental habits, many friends, love troubles, death under distressing circumstances.

With Neptune. Strong character, firm, occult interests, mental disturbance at end of life, connected with societies, success in business connected with clothing or ornaments, success in dealing with opposite sex, domestic harmony, accumulates wealth, sudden death.

59. HAN. ʒ *Ophiuchi.* ♐ 8° 7'.
Notes. A small star situated near the left knee of Ophiuchus.

Influence. Of the nature of Saturn and Venus. It brings trouble and disgrace.

With Sun. Sickness, disgrace and ruin.

With Moon. Disgrace, ruin, and ailments affecting those parts ruled by Sagittarius.

60. ISIDIS. δ *Scorpii.* ♐ 1° 27′.

Notes. Situated near the right claw of the Scorpion.

Influence. According to Ptolemy it is of the nature of Mars and Saturn ; and, to Alvidas, of Jupiter in square to the Moon. It causes sudden assaults, malevolence, immorality and shamelessness.

With Sun. Immoral, dissipated, low associates, many sorrows.

With Moon. Reserved, suspicious, bad for business success, disgrace, loss by horses and cattle.

With Mercury. Hypocritical, evil mind, low associates, imprisonment, malignant disease but chances of recovery, criminal, secrets in connection with life or parentage, domestic disharmony.

With Venus. Quiet, reserved, jealous, selfish, favourable for gain.

With Mars. Immoral, criminal, violent, evil environment, sudden or violent death.

With Jupiter. Deceitful, dishonest, dissipated, low companions, danger of imprisonment.

With Saturn. Vacillating, strong passions, evil habits, low associates, may be disowned by family, several unhappy marriages, early death of favourite child, death from consumption.

With Uranus. Shrewd, cunning, excellent linguist, bad morals, trouble through opposite sex, bad for marriage, many enemies, strange adventures abroad—sometimes as spy, bad for gain, obscure death.

With Neptune. Active mind, weak character, easily led, ruined through opposite sex, organizing ability, high position but subsequent disgrace, accidents from fire, water and electricity, death by accident or by human hands.

61. KHAMBALIA. λ *Virginis.* ♏ 5° 45′.

Notes. A small star situated on the left foot of Virgo. From the Coptic meaning Crooked-clawed.

Influence. Of the nature of Mercury and Mars. It causes swift violence, unreliability, changeability, and an argumentative nature.

62. LABRUM. δ *Crateris.* ♍ 25° 35′.

Notes. Situated in the Cup, and symbolically called the Holy Grail.

Influence. Of the nature of Venus and Mercury. It gives ideality, psychic power, intelligence, honour and riches in disgrace and purifies to salvation.

If rising. Ecclesiastical preferment, or very good fortune.

63. LESATH. υ *Scorpii.* ♐ 22° 54′.

Notes. A small star situated on the sting of the Scorpion. From Al Las'ah, the Sting.

Influence. Of the nature of Mercury and Mars. It gives danger, desperation, immorality and malevolence, and is connected with acid poisons.

64. MANUBRIUM. ο *Sagittarii.* ♑ 13° 52′.

Notes. Part of the cluster in the Archer's Face

Influence. Of the nature of the Sun and Mars. It causes blindness, explosions, fire, flaring heat heroism, courage, and defiance.

65. MARKAB. α *Pegasi.* ♓ 22° 22'.

Notes. A white star situated on the wing of Pegasus. From Markab, a Saddle, Ship or Vehicle, or, according to Bullinger, Returning from Afar.

Influence. According to Ptolemy it is of the nature of Mars and Mercury ; to Simmonite, of Mars and Venus ; and, to Alvidas, of Jupiter in square to Mercury with Saturn from Pisces and Gemini. It gives honour, riches, fortune, danger from fevers, cuts, blows, stabs and fire and a violent death.

If culminating. Disgrace, ruin and often a violent death.

With Sun. Energetic, unlucky, impermanent martial honours, disappointed ambitions, accidents, sickness.

With Moon. Injuries from enemies, bad for gain and domestic matters, fairly good health but many accidents. If Mars be with Moon, death by wild beasts or soldiers. If a malefic be with Cingula Orionis, death by human hands.

With Mercury. Good mind, rash and headstrong, quick in speech, diplomatic, capable writer, criticized, friends become enemies, bad for gain.

With Venus. Evil associates, drink and other excesses, bad for gain.

With Mars. Quarrelsome, violent, many difficulties and losses through Mercurial affairs.

With Jupiter. Trouble and loss through legal

aatters, danger of judicial sentence or banishment and exile.

With Saturn. Born in poverty, prison or asylum, may be abandoned, hard life, imprisoned for crime, few friends, unfavourable for domestic matters, death under similar conditions to birth.

With Uranus. Evil habits, mental disturbances, clever, wanderer, unavailing efforts, peculiar life, trouble with parent of opposite sex, bad for gain and domestic matters, many accidents, violent death.

With Neptune. Unbalanced or abnormal mind, many disappointments, emotional, romantic, distasteful environment, secret enemies, domestic disharmony, many accidents, violent death in early life.

With a malefic and the Moon at the same time with Cingula Orionis, death by drowning.

66. MARKEB. κ *Argus.* ♍ 27° 48'.

Notes. A small star in the Buckler of the Ship.

Influence. Of the nature of Saturn and Jupiter. It gives piety, a wide knowledge, educational work and voyages.

If rising. Profitable journeys in company with Jupiterian and Saturnian people wherein native is grave and discreet but suffers much injury which ultimately turns to good.

67. MENKALINAN. β *Aurigæ.* ♊ 28° 48'.

Notes. A bright yellow star situated on the right shoulder of Auriga. From Al Mankib dhi'l Inan, the Shoulder of the Rein-holder.

Influence. Of the nature of Mars and Mercury.

It causes ruin, disgrace, and frequently violent death.

68. MENKAR. α *Ceti*. ♉ 13° 12′.

Notes. A bright orange star situated in the jaw of the Whale. From Al Minhar, the Nose.

Influence. According to Ptolemy it is of the nature of Saturn ; to Simmonite, of Mars ; and, to Alvidas, of Venus and the Moon. It causes disease, disgrace, ruin, injury from beasts, sickness, and loss of fortune.

If rising. Legacies and inheritances attended by much evil.

If culminating. Disgrace, ruin, danger from cattle and large beasts.

With Sun. Great trouble, sickness, throat ailments, legacies and inheritances attended by much evil, loss of money, failure of crops.

With Moon. Mental anxiety, hatred of the vulgar, ill-will of women, danger from thieves, sickness to native and family, loss of marriage partner or near relative, quarrels, legal losses, legacies and inheritances attended by much evil.

With Mercury. Difficulties through writings, difficulty in payment of mortgages, bad for gain, ill-health to marriage partner or relative, destruction of crops.

With Venus. Strong and uncontrolled passions, jealousy, domestic disharmony and temporary separation, ill-health of marriage partner.

With Mars. Evil associates, immoral, violent, murderous, violent death.

With Jupiter. Deceitful, dishonest, wandering life, imprisonment, banishment, or judicial sentence.

With Saturn. Self-seeking, selfish, causes un-happiness to others, much sickness, bad for gain.

With Uranus. Active mind, artistic, scientific and mystical interest and ability, troubles through opposite sex, loss through fire and false friends, good fortune and misfortune alternately, severe injuries from animals.

With Neptune. Peculiar early life, loss of or separa-tion from parents abroad, may lose identity and be brought up by foreigners in dishonour, learns of parentage too late in life to obtain advantage, brave, organizing ability, high position, wasted talents, many journeys, violent death frequently by assas-sination.

69. MINTAKA. δ *Orionis.* ♊ 21° 16′.

Notes. A slightly variable double star, brilliant white and pale violet situated in Orion's belt. From Al Mintakah, the Belt, or Dividing.

Influence. According to Ptolemy it is of the nature of Saturn and Mercury; and, to Alvidas, of Mercury, Saturn and Jupiter. It gives good fortune.

With Sun. Discreet, cautious, somewhat change-able.

With Moon. Active, sharp, alert in business, public position, many enemies, more successful in business.

With Mercury. Studious, fond of seclusion, deliberate and fixed mind, little sympathy or dis-agreements with relatives, bad for gain.

With Venus. Public position, enmity of women, love disappointments.

With Mars. Energetic, quick mind, good speaker and debater, quarrelsome, strong passions.

With Jupiter. High position in law or Church, studious and philosophical mind, gain through inheritance.

With Saturn. Far-seeing, studious, good judge of human nature, psychic, domestic disharmony, sickness to family.

With Uranus. Selfish, studious, eccentric, difficult to get on with, losses through lawsuits and business, successful in middle age but poverty at end of life, favourable for domestic matters, death from consumption.

With Neptune. Thoughtful, studious, keeps discoveries to himself, sarcastic writer, generous but not wealthy, rarely marries, death unattended in old age.

(See CINGULA ORIONIS).

70. MIRACH. β *Andromedœ.* ♈ 29° 17′.

Notes. A yellow star situated in the girdle of Andromeda. From Mirak, the Loins. Often called Zona Andromedæ, or Andromeda's Girdle.

Influence. According to Ptolemy it is of the nature of Venus ; and, to Alvidas, of Mars and the Moon. It gives personal beauty, a brilliant mind, a love of home, great devotion, beneficence, forgiveness, love, overcoming by kindness, renown, and good fortune in marriage.

With Sun. Trouble through opposite sex, disappointments in expectations but otherwise favourable.

With Moon. Trouble with opposite sex owing

to indiscretions, bad for domestic affairs, honour through martial matters.

With Mercury. Vacillating, unstable, peculiar events, many travels and changes, little success.

With Venus. Voluptuous, bad morals, scandal, drink or drug-taking late in life.

With Mars. Ill-mannered, boisterous, evil associations, may be tramp.

With Jupiter. Help from women but danger of scandal, much travel, legal or ecclesiastical difficulties.

With Saturn. Strong passions, debauchery, mechanical genius, misdirected talents.

With Uranus. Unbalanced mind, may commit crime in insanity, occult interests, continual disappointments, bad for domestic affairs, peculiar or violent death.

With Neptune. Persevering, ambitious, strong passions, eccentric, dishonest, domestic disharmony and separation, may disinherit children or family, trouble through companies and inventions, successful business, many enemies and few friends, painful and lingering death.

71. NASHIRA. γ *Capricorni.* ♒ 20° 40'.

Notes. Situated in the tail of the Goat. From Al Sa'd al Nashirah, the Fortunate One or Bringer of Good Tidings ; or, according to Bullinger, the Record of the Cutting Off.

Influence. According to Ptolemy it is of the nature of Saturn and Jupiter ; and, to Simmonite, of Saturn. It causes overcoming by evil, which is turned to success, and gives danger from beasts.

72. OCULUS. π *Capricorni.* ♒ 3° 36′.
Notes. A small star in the right eye of the Goat.
Influence. Of the nature of Saturn and Venus. It gives a clever and piercing intellect when in conjunction with Mercury.

73. PELAGUS. σ *Sagittarii.* ♑ 11° 16′.
Notes. A small star situated on the vane of the arrow at the Archer's hand.
Influence. According to Ptolemy it is of the nature of Jupiter and Mercury ; and, to Alvidas, of Saturn and Mercury. It gives truthfulness, optimism and a religious mind.
With Sun. Influential public position, favourable for domestic and family matters.
With Moon. Successful writer on science, philosophy, education or agriculture, unorthodox in religion, defeats enemies, many friends, illness of a Saturnian nature.
With Mercury. High government position, popular criticism, wealth, anxiety on account of illness to wife or mother.
With Venus. Heart rules head, favours from opposite sex, many friends.
With Mars. Reserved, diplomatic, strong mind, courageous, energetic, straightforward, false friends, favourable for gain.
With Jupiter. Diplomatic, philosophical mind, writer, ecclesiastical or legal preferment.
With Saturn. Thoughtful, reserved, self-centred, success delayed until after 50, ambition thwarted by enemies, danger of disgrace, wealth at end of life,

trouble to parents, favourable marriage late in life, usually at least one child.

With Uranus. Proud, industrious, aggressive, high government or business position, early disgrace, especially if female, favourable for marriage in middle age, sudden gains and losses, many friends, natural death.

With Neptune. Practical, occult interests, wealthy, associated with large concerns, some domestic disagreements, defeats enemies, natural death in old age.

74. PHACT. α *Columbæ.* ♊ 21° 3′.

Notes. Situated at the base of the right wing of the Dove. Said to be from Had'ar, Ground, or Fached, the Thigh.

Influence. Of the nature of Venus and Mercury. It gives beneficence, hopefulness and good fortune.

75. PLEIADES. In the neighbourhood of ♉ 28° 52′. (See ALCYONE.)

Legend. The Pleiades or Atlantides were the seven daughters of Atlas and Pleione, six of whom are described as visible, and one as invisible or " lost." They were the virgin companions of Diana, and were translated into heaven in order to escape the importunities of Orion, or according to another account because of their grief at the fate of their father, Atlas, who was condemned to support the weight of the heavens on his head and hands.

The names of the sisters, and the catalogue numbers of the stars representing them are as follows :—Alcyone (η), Maia (20), Electra (17),

Merope (23), Taygete (19), Celæno (16), and Sterope (21 and 22), and to these have been added the parents, Atlas (27) and Pleione (28).

The missing or lost Pleiad has been said to be Merope, who alone married a mortal, Sisyphus, and hid her face in shame at being the only one not married to a god, but other accounts substitute either Electra, who withdrew her light in sorrow at the destruction of Ilium, which was founded by her son Dardanos ; or Celæno, which Theon the Younger said was struck by lightning.

Notes. The Pleiades form a cluster, with Alcyone as the principal star, situated on the shoulder of the Bull. For all practical purposes the longitude of Alcyone may be used for the whole group, as all are contained within about one degree of longitude.

Influence. According to Ptolemy they are of the nature of the Moon and Mars ; and, to Alvidas, of Mars, Moon and Sun in opposition. They are said to make their natives wanton, ambitious, turbulent, optimistic and peaceful ; to give many journeys and voyages, success in agriculture and through active intelligence; and to cause blindness, disgrace and a violent death. Their influence is distinctly evil and there is no astrological warrant for the oft-quoted passage in Job (xxxviii. 31), " Canst thou bind the sweet influences of Pleiades . . . ? " which is probably a mistranslation.

If rising. Blindness, ophthalmia, injuries to the eyes and face, disgrace, wounds, stabs, exile, imprisonment, sickness, violent fevers, quarrels, violent lust, military preferment. If at the same time the

Sun is in opposition either to the Ascendant or to Mars, violent death.

If culminating. Disgrace, ruin, violent death. If with the luminaries it makes its natives military captains, commanders, colonels of horse and emperors.

With Sun. Throat ailments, chronic catarrh, blindness, bad eyes, injuries to the face, sickness, disgrace, evil disposition, murderer or murdered, imprisonment, death by pestilence, blows, stabs, shooting, beheading or shipwreck. If in 7th house, blindness, especially if Saturn or Mars be with Regulus. If with Mars and Venus the native will be a potent king obeyed by many people but subject to many infirmities.

With Moon. Injuries to the face, sickness, misfortune, wounds, stabs, disgrace, imprisonment, blindness, defective sight especially if in the Ascendant or one of the other angles, may be cross-eyed, colour-blind or the eyes may be affected by some growth. If in the 7th house, total blindness especially if Saturn or Mars be with Regulus and the Moon be combust.

With Mercury. Many disappointments, loss of possessions, much loss from legal affairs, business failure, trouble through children.

With Venus. Immoral, strong passions, disgrace through women, sickness, loss of fortune.

With Mars. Many accidents to the head, loss and suffering through fires. If at the same time Saturn is with Regulus, violent death in a tumult.

With Jupiter. Deceit, hypocrisy, legal and ecclesiastical troubles, loss through relatives, banishment or imprisonment.

With Saturn. Cautious, much sickness, tumorous ailments, chronic sickness to family, many losses.

With Uranus. Active mind, deformity from birth or through accident in childhood, many accidents and troubles, many unexpected losses often through fire or enemies, marriage partner proves false especially if female, troubles through women, occult interests, unfavourable for children, if any, and lack of harmony with them, heavy losses at end of life, violent death.

With Neptune. Bold, military preferment, honour, wealth, help from friends, many serious accidents, many travels, somewhat dishonourable occupation involving secrecy, ill-health to marriage partner and peculiar conditions respecting parentage, bad for children, may lose everything at end of life, violent death, often abroad while following occupation.

76. POLARIS. *a Ursæ Minoris.* ♊ 27° 27′.

Notes. A double star, topaz yellow and pale white, situated in the tail of the Lesser Bear, and marking the celestial pole. Also called Al Rukkabah, the Riders ; Cynosura, the Dog's Tail ; and Stella Polaris, the Pole Star. Owing to the precession of the equinoxes the pole moves in a circle among the stars taking about 26,000 years to complete one revolution. At present Polaris is 1° 14′ distant from the pole and will continue to approach it until the year 2095 when it will reach its nearest distance of 26′ 30″ and then recede. The chief stars that will mark the position of the pole are successively as follows :— γ, π, ζ, ν, and a

Cephei ; α and δ Cygni ; α Lyræ ; ι and τ Herculis ; θ, ι, and α Draconis ; β Ursæ Minoris; κ Draconis ; and then α Ursæ Minoris, our Polaris, again. About the year 12,200 B.C., α Lyræ (Wega) marked the pole ; ι Draconis about 4,500 B.C. ; and α Draconis about 2,700 B.C. ; while γ Cephei will occupy this position in about 4,500 A.D. ; α Cephei in 7,500 A.D. ; δ Cygni in 11,300 A.D. ; and Wega in about 13,500 A.D.

Influence. Of the nature of Saturn and Venus. It causes much sickness, trouble, loss of fortune, disgrace and great affliction, and may give legacies and inheritances attended by much evil. The Arabs were of the opinion that the contemplation of Polaris cured ophthalmia.

With Sun. Many troubles and evils.

With Moon. Hatred of the vulgar, ill-will of women and danger from thieves.

77. POLIS. μ *Sagittarii.* ♑ 2° 6′.

Notes. A triple star in the upper part of the bow of Sagittarius. From the Coptic Polis, a Foal.

Influence. Of the nature of Jupiter and Mars. It gives success, high ambition, martial desires, horsemanship, keen perception and domination.

78. POLLUX. β *Geminorum.* ♋ 22° 7′.

Notes. An orange star situated on the head of the Southern Twin. It represents Pollux, son of Jupiter and Leda, and the immortal one of the twins, famous for his skill in boxing. Sometimes called Hercules, and symbolically named A Heartless Judge.

Influence. According to Ptolemy it is of the nature of Mars ; and, to Alvidas, of the Moon, Mars and Uranus. It gives a subtle, crafty, spirited, brave, audacious, cruel and rash nature, a love of boxing, dignified malevolence, and is connected with poisons.

If rising. Bad eyes, blindness, injuries to the face, sickness, wounds, imprisonment, ephemeral honour and preferment.

If culminating. Honour and preferment but danger of disgrace and ruin.

With Sun. Occult and philosophical interests, blows, stabs, serious accidents, shooting, shipwreck, murderer or murdered, extreme sickness and diseases, fevers, ailments affecting the stomach, evil disposition, riches and honour but final ruin, blindness, injuries to the head and face, quarrels, rape committed or suffered, banishment, imprisonment for embezzling, violent death, decapitation.

With Moon. Hatred of the vulgar, ill-will of women, danger from thieves, violent death, power, pride, sickness, calamity, wounds, imprisonment, injuries to face, defective sight or blindness especially if Mars or the Sun be in square from Aries. If Mars or the Sun be in square from Libra, danger of accidents and legal or matrimonial troubles ; but, if in opposition from Capricorn, danger to the mother's honour and reputation. If Mars be in conjunction, death by suffocation, drowning or assassination. If Mars be with Arcturus in the 1st, 7th, 9th, 10th or 11th houses, death by suffocation.

With Mercury. Unbalanced mind, unpopular and peculiar occupation, trouble with father through relatives or enemies, domestic disharmony, anxiety, loss through land, property and mines.

With Venus. Strong and irregulated passions, danger of seduction if female, loss through women, danger of poison.

With Mars. Violent, murderer or murdered, high position but final ruin, violent death by suffocation, drowning or assassination especially if the Moon be there also.

With Jupiter. Legal losses, high position but danger of disgrace, trouble through relatives, banishment or imprisonment.

With Saturn. Bad temper, bitter, sarcastic, loss of arm or leg, loss of parents or trouble through stepparents, much help from a friend, lack of education, sudden death while following occupation through horses or large animals.

With Uranus. Occult interests, psychic ability, selfish, proud, vain of personal appearance, success in connection with the Government, companies or electrical matters, harmonious marriage in middle age, favourable for children, end of life not so favourable as middle.

With Neptune. Changeable, many travels, excellent linguist, many influential friends, good for partnership, peculiar conditions in marriage and partner often a foreigner, occupation connected with exploration or zoological and botanical work abroad, minor accidents, isolated death through fever or virulent disease.

79. PRÆSÆPE. *44 M Cancri.* ♋ 6° 7′.
Legend. Præsæpe represents the manger of the asses ridden by Bacchus and Vulcan (see ASELLI).
Notes. A coarse extended cluster situated on the

head of the Crab. Popularly termed the Beehive, Manger or Crib, and known by the Chinese under the name Tseih She Ke, Exhalation of Piled-up Corpses. With the Aselli it was the " cloudy spot of Cancer " mentioned by Ptolemy as causing blindness

Influence. It is of the nature of Mars and the Moon, and causes disease, disgrace, adventure, insolence, wantonness, brutality, blindness, industry, order and fecundity ; and makes its natives fortunate though liable to loss through others, and the founders of large businesses.

If rising. Blindness especially of the left eye, ophthalmia, injuries to the face, sickness, violent fevers, wounds in face and arms, stabs, violent lust, imprisonment, exile. If at the same time the Sun opposes Mars or the Ascendant, violent death.

If culminating. Disgrace, ruin and violent death.

With Sun. Evil disposition, murderer or murdered, blows, stabs, serious accidents, shooting, shipwreck, execution, banishment, imprisonment, sharp diseases, fevers, hæmorrhage, lawsuits, danger of death from fire, iron or stones, injuries to the face, wounds, bad eyes, and if in an angle blindness.

With Moon. Wounds, stabs, imprisonment, injuries to the face, sickness, blindness or eye injuries especially if Saturn or Mars be with Regulus.

80. PRIMA HYADUM. γ *Tauri.* Π 4° 41′.
(The chief star of the Hyades).

Legend. The Hyades were the seven daughters of Atlas and Æthra, half-sisters of the Pleiades, with whom they were entrusted by Jupiter with the care of the infant Bacchus. They were placed among the stars as a reward for their sisterly love which was evinced by their sorrow at the death of their brother Hyas, who was killed by a wild beast in Libya.

Notes. The Hyades consist of six stars (α, θ^1, θ^2, γ, δ, and ϵ, Tauri) situated on the forehead of the Bull and marking the northern eye.

Influence. According to Ptolemy they are of the nature of Saturn and Mercury ; and, to Alvidas, of Mercury and Mars. Simmonite likens this them to Mars but this is probably a misinterpretation of Ptolemy's meaning. They give tears, sudden events, violence, fierceness, poisoning, blindness, wounds or injuries to the head by instruments, weapons or fevers, and contradictions of fortune.

If rising. Blindness, bad eyes, injuries to the face, wounds, stabs, imprisonment.

If culminating. Disgrace, ruin, violent death.

If rising or culminating with luminaries, make their natives military captains, commanders, colonels of horse and emperors.

With Sun. Evil disposition, disturbed mind, failure in study, muddled thinking, misfortune, murderer or murdered, death by blows, stabs, shooting, beheading or shipwreck.

With Moon. Tactful, fair ability, difficulties connected with writings, may forge the name of employer or friend but finally escape punishment and retain position, liable to sickness and disgrace, danger of blindness or eye injuries.

With Mercury. Quick mind, resentful, hasty temper, broods over small troubles, favourable for gain.

With Venus. Many accomplishments, artistic, ability to write or paint, strong passions which influence work.

With Mars. Abrupt, brave, aggressive, courageous, lacks concentration.

With Jupiter. Ambitious, dishonest, legal difficulties, quarrels with relatives, judicial sentence.

With Saturn. Caution, forethought, omnivorous reader, scientific, success but little prominence, worry and annoyance from relatives.

With Uranus. Scientific, literary, artistic and mystical interests, unconsciously psychic, greatly influenced by environment, favourable for marriage after 35 and for gain and children, ill-health, seldom long life.

With Neptune. Keen intellect, learned, kind-hearted, sympathetic, scientific and philosophical interests, some inventive genius often connected with etheric, waves, which will bring fame but not wealth, broad and unorthodox religious views, benefits from companies, favourable for domestic matters, not good for children, brothers or sisters, knowledge gained psychically, sudden death while engaged in important work.

81. PRINCEPS. *δ Boötis.* ♏ 2° 2′.

Notes. A pale yellow star situated in the spear-shaft of Boötes.

Influence. Of the nature of Mercury and Saturn. It gives a keen, studious and profound mind, with the ability for research.

If rising. Good fortune, but troubles, discontent and fear occasioned by own temerity rather than circumstances.

82. PROCYON. α *Canis Minoris.* ♋ 24° 41'.

Notes. A binary yellowish white and yellow star situated on the body of the Lesser Dog. From Prokuon, before the Dog, in allusion to its rising before Sirius.

Influence. According to Ptolemy it is of the nature of Mercury and Mars; to Simmonite, of Venus and Mars, which is probably a misprint; and, to Alvidas, of the Moon, Jupiter and Uranus. It gives activity, violence, sudden and violent malevolence, sudden preferment by exertion, elevation ending in disaster, danger of dog bites and hydrophobia, and makes its natives petulant, saucy, giddy, weak-natured, timid, unfortunate, proud, easily angered, careless and violent. Two cases are on record of death or injury by dog bite in which Procyon and Sirius are involved.

1. Male, born 14th September, 1829, 54° N. Died from the bite of a dog. Sirius was in square to the Moon and also to Mercury in the 8th house, while Procyon was in square to Venus in the 8th. The ascendant fell midway between the opposition of both stars.

2. Male, born 6th July, 1885, 6.15 p.m., 54° N. 3', 2° W. 46'. Bitten in the leg by a dog on 9th December, 1901, and was not expected to live. Sirius was in conjunction with the Sun near the cusp of the 8th house, and Procyon was in conjunction with Mercury within that house.

If rising. Artful, crafty, dissembling, wealth by violence and rapine, lust, dissipation, waste and ruin, military preferment, quarrels, loss in trade or by servants.

With Sun. Great help from friends, gifts and legacies if not afflicted, military preferment after great struggles and expense. If rising or culminating, kingly preferment.

With Moon. Occult interests, restless, never remains long in one place, quarrels with friends, partners and employers. If at the same time the Sun and Mars be with Deneb Adige or Wega, above the earth, death from the bite of a mad dog.

With Mercury. Occult interest, minor position of management under Government, trouble and scandal through opposite sex, favourable for health and gain.

With Venus. Many benefits from influential friends, associated with the Church, favourable for gain.

With Mars. Cruelty, violence, scandal and slander, disgrace and ruin, danger of dog bites.

With Jupiter. Many journeys, trouble through relatives and the Church or law, help from friends.

With Saturn. Good judgment, high position of trust often in connection with land, may be adopted by aged couple from whom a good inheritance is obtained, benefits from elderly friends, good health, domestic harmony, marriage to one of higher station.

With Uranus. Broad-minded, liberal, minister or speaker on religious and philosophical subjects, not limited to any definite creed, many friends among the people, favourable for domestic matters.

With Neptune. Sensitive and mediumistic, notorious through and luck in speculation, political interests, wealthy friends, favourable for domestic matters, death from tumorous growth after unsuccessful operation leaving financial affairs involved.

83. PROPUS. *ι Geminorum.* ♋ 17° 50'.

Notes. A small star situated between the shoulders of the Twins.

Influence. Of the nature of Mercury and Venus. It gives strength, eminence and success.

84. RASALHAGUE. *α Ophiuchi.* ♐ 21° 20'.

Notes. A sapphire star situated on the head of Ophiuchus. From Ras al Hawwa, the Head of the Serpent Charmer.

Influence. According to Ptolemy it is of the nature of Saturn and Venus ; and, to Alvidas, of Jupiter and Mercury in sextile to Mars. It gives misfortune through women, perverted tastes and mental depravity.

With Sun. Reserved, thoughtful, studious, suspicious, solitary, reputation for athletics, little wealth, careless of public opinion.

With Moon. Public prominence in religious matters, favourable for gain.

With Mercury. Unpopular attitude and criticism through religion, philosophy or science; difficulties in marriage and quarrels fostered by others, trouble through opposite sex, not very good for gain.

With Venus. Quick mind, well educated, cautious, secretive, suspicious, unfavourable for gain.

With Mars. Trouble through writings, public censure in connection with religion, science or philosophy, bad for gain.

With Jupiter. Diplomatic, religious or legal preferment, but some criticism, favourable for gain.

With Saturn. Selfish, unpopular, determined, fixed opinions, successful, somewhat dishonest, domestic disharmony through jealousy, marriage partner may be invalid, losses of a Mercurial nature.

With Uranus. Strong passions, strong nature but changeable, ambitious, occult interests, seeks popularity, easily swayed though outwardly aggressive, reverence for ancestry, benefits through elderly and influential people and public affairs, unfavourable for marriage and children, if any, trouble through opposite sex, sudden death.

With Neptune. Hypocritical, self-seeking, able speaker or writer, but panders to the public, occult, religious or scientific work, but largely misleading, minor Government position, domestic disharmony, ill-health to marriage partner, disappointment over legacy, peculiar death sometimes through fall but animal and human agency may be suspected.

85. RASTABAN. *β Draconis*. ♐ 10° 50'.

Notes. A binary yellow star situated in the head of the Dragon, and anciently called " The Nebulous Star in the Dragon's Eye." From Al Ras al Thuban, the Dragon's Head.

Influence. Of the nature of Saturn and Mars. It gives loss of property, violence, criminal inclinations and accidents.

With Moon. Blindness, wounds, quarrels, bruises, stabs, blows and kicks from horses.

86. REGULUS. *α Leonis*. ♌ 28° 43'.

Notes. A triple star, flushed white and ultramarine, situated on the body of the Lion. From Regulus, a Little King, and often called Cor Leonis, the Lion's Heart, and symbolically the Crushing Foot. It was one of the four Royal Stars of the Persians in 3,000 B.C., when, as Watcher of the North, it marked the summer solstice.

Influence. According to Ptolemy it is of the nature of Mars and Jupiter, but most later authors liken it to Mars only, while Alvidas states that it is similar to the Sun in good aspect to Uranus. It gives violence, destructiveness, military honour of short duration, with ultimate failure, imprisonment, violent death, success, high and lofty ideals and strength of spirit, and makes its natives magnanimous, grandly liberal, generous, ambitious, fond of power, desirous of command, high-spirited and independent.

If rising. Great honour and wealth, but violence and trouble, sickness, fevers, acute diseases, benefits seldom last, favour of the great, victory over enemies and scandal. The 145th Consideration of Guido Bonatus is as follows :—" That thou see in Diurnal Nativities whether Cor Leonis be in the Ascendant, that is to say, in the Oriental Line or above it one degree or below it three degrees ; or whether it be in the tenth in like degrees, without the Conjunction or Aspect of any of the Fortunes ; for this alone signifies that the Native shall be a person of great note and power, too much exalted, and attain to high preferment and honours, although descended from the meanest parents. And, if any of the Fortunes behold that place also, his glory shall be the more increased ; but, if the Nativity be nocturnal, his fortune will be somewhat meaner, but not much ; but if the Infortunes cast their aspects there it will still be more mean ; but if the Fortunes behold it also they will augment the good promised a fourth part, and mitigate the evil as much ; yet still, whatever of all this happens, it signifies that the Native shall die an unhappy death ; or at least that all his honours, greatness and power shall at last suffer an eclipse and set in a cloud."

If culminating. Honour, preferment, good fortune, high office under Government, military success. If with Sun, Moon or Jupiter, great honour and ample fortune.

With Sun. Power, authority, great influence over friends, honour and riches, but violence, trouble and ultimate disgrace and ruin, sickness, fevers, benefits seldom last.

With Moon. Occult interests, powerful friends, danger from enemies and false friends, gain by speculation, public prominence, great power, honour, wealth, benefits seldom last, violence, trouble and sickness. Makes women high-spirited and independent. If at the same time the Sun is with the Dragon's Head in Gemini, or Jupiter is in the 10th house in trine to Mars and the Sun is with the Dragon's Head, great preferment even from the lowest sphere to high rank.

With Mercury. Honourable, just, popular, generosity abused by opponents, fame, gain through high position.

With Venus. Many disappointments, unexpected happenings, violent attachments, trouble through love affairs.

With Mars. Honour, fame, strong character, public prominence, high military command.

With Jupiter. Fame, high preferment, especially of a military nature, success in the Church.

With Saturn. Just, friends among clergy, success in Church or law, scholarly, wealth, gain through speculation, companies and friends, high position, proud of home and family, good health, heart trouble at end of life. If angular and especially if rising or culminating, public honour and credit. If Mars be with the Pleiades, violent death in a tumult.

With Uranus. Energetic, ambitious, successful, may be unjust or dishonourable, self-aggrandisement, high official position, panders to aristocracy, associated with religion for business purposes, gain through speculation and companies, favourable for marriage, sorrow through death of daughter and disappointment through a son, friends become enemies at end of life, may retire and live in seclusion, violent death through accident or assassination.

With Neptune. Prominent leader, law-giver, diplomatic, strong character, control over others, influential friends, few if any enemies, domestic harmony, natural death in old age.

With a malefic and the Moon with Antares, Præsæpe or the Pleiades, blindness or injuries to the eyes.

87. RIGEL. *β Orionis.* ♊ 15° 43'.

Notes. A double bluish white star situated on the left foot of Orion. From Rijl, the Foot.

Influence. According to Ptolemy and Lilly it is of the nature of Jupiter and Saturn, but later authors consider it favourable and similar to Jupiter and Mars. Alvidas likens it to Mercury, Mars and Jupiter. It gives benevolence, honour, riches, happiness, glory, renown and inventive or mechanical ability.

If rising. Good fortune, preferment, riches, great and lasting honours.

If culminating. Great military or ecclesiastical preferment, anger, vexation, magnanimity, much gain acquired by labour and mental anxiety, lasting honours.

With Sun. Bold, courageous, insolent, unruly temper, hasty actions, bloodshed, many enemies, great good fortune, military success.

With Moon. Much worry and disappointment, injuries to life and fortune, sickness, bad for gain, ill-health or death to wife or mother.

With Mercury. Scientific, prominent position in connection with Mercurial matters or in science.

With Venus. Honours or favours in middle life, good and influential marriage especially if female.

With Mars. Unruly, ingenious, occupied with mechanical matters, great military preferment.

With Jupiter. Great legal or ecclesiastical preferment, many journeys, benefits from foreign affairs, favourable for marriage.

With Saturn. Benefits from elderly people, clergy and lawyers, just, discriminative, good for legacy and inheritance, domestic harmony, good health, long life.

With Uranus. Scientific, romantic, interested in antiquities, fame through historical or geological discoveries, probably in an unexplored country, friendships formed in a peculiar way abroad, many adventures and narrow escapes, early love disappointment, favourable for marriage after 30, death through some trivial accident abroad.

With Neptune. Kind, energetic, scholarly and active mind, position under Government or at the head of some learned institution, cautious, reserved, resourceful, prompt, diplomatic, occult interests, success, public prominence, domestic harmony, natural death.

88. SABIK. η *Ophiuchi.* ♐ 16° 51′.

Notes. A pale yellow star situated on the left knee of Ophiuchus. From Sabik, Preceding One.

Influence. According to Ptolemy it is of the nature of Saturn and Venus ; and, to Alvidas, of Jupiter and Venus. It causes wastefulness, lost energy, perverted morals, and success in evil deeds.

With Sun. Sincere, honourable, scientific, religious and philosophical interests, unorthodox or heretical, moral courage, bad for gain.

With Moon. Secret enmity and jealousy, trouble through relatives, successful but not wealthy, success in breeding stock.

With Mercury. Injury from open enemies, little help from friends, failure in business, fairly good for gain but legal losses, scandal through relatives of marriage partner.

With Venus. Musical and artistic ability, not very favourable for gain.

With Mars. Unorthodox or heretical religious views that may cause trouble, domestic disharmony, trouble through love affairs, bad for gain.

With Jupiter. Material success, preferment in

Church or law but criticized, gain through large animals, trouble through relatives.

With Saturn. Industrious, persevering, economical, strong passions, trouble through some active indiscretion affecting whole life, trouble and disappointment in love affairs, secret help from female friends which may cause scandal, success especially in latter part of life in affairs of an earthy or Sagittarian nature, but little prominence.

With Uranus. Sincere, sober, retiring, melancholy, thoughtful, calm and patient in trouble, clergyman or associated with the Church, some physical disability, separated from friends and relatives, some great sorrow in the life, occupied in doing good but disappointed in results, rarely marries.

With Neptune. Highly sensitive, psychic, strong will, prominent writer or speaker, success, many friends, favours from opposite sex, gifts and legacies used for scientific purposes, domestic harmony, sudden death in middle age from colds or consumption.

89. SADALMELIK. α *Aquarii.* ⋈ 2° 14'.

Notes. A pale yellow star situated on the right shoulder of Aquarius. From Al Sa'd al Malik, the Lucky One of the King.

Influence. According to Ptolemy it is of the nature of Saturn and Mercury ; to Simmonite, of Saturn and Jupiter ; and to Alvidas of Jupiter and Uranus in sextile to the Sun from Pisces and Taurus. It causes persecution, lawsuits, extreme and sudden destruction and the death penalty.

With Sun. Occult interests, prominence in occultism, gain through companies.

With Moon. Prominence in occult matters, success in large companies, favourable for gain. If at the same time a malefic be with Algol, death by royal command either by hanging or by decapitation.

With Mercury. Occult interests and research, criticized, favourable for friendship, success in large companies, loss through servants.

With Venus. Favourable for occult investigation, gain through friends.

With Mars. Fame through discoveries in science or inventions, benefits do not last.

With Jupiter. Ecclesiastical success, occult interests, criticized, trouble through enemies, loss through lawsuits.

With Saturn. Original, inventive, psychic, careful, cautious, practical, good judgment, difficulty in putting ideas or inventions into practice, gain through companies, speculation and matters of an earthy nature, chronic illness to wife or children, favourable for gain, long life.

With Uranus. High ideals, philosophical, scientific, good mind, psychic, inventive, successful, gain through business or under Government, influential and learned friends, does much good in purifying creeds and philosophies, sudden but natural death.

With Neptune. Psychic, prominence in occult matters, kind, sympathetic, generous, friends among clergy and lawyers, favourable for gain through companies, banks or stocks, domestic harmony but sickness to wife or children entailing the breaking up of home, minor accidents, long life.

90. SADALSUUD. β *Aquarii*. ≈≈ 22° 17′.

Notes. A pale yellow star situated on the left shoulder of Aquarius. From Al Sa'd al Suud, the Luckiest of the Lucky, so called on account of its heliacal rising marking the period of gentle and continuous rain.

Influence. According to Ptolemy it is of the nature of Saturn and Mercury; to Simmonite, of Uranus; and, to Alvidas, of Uranus in sextile to the Sun. It is said to cause trouble and disgrace.

With Sun. Occult interests, psychic, wealth through opposite sex involving litigation, domestic harmony.

With Moon. Reputation through occult matters, respect of friends, favourable for gain, peculiar domestic conditions.

With Mercury. Social success, favours from opposite sex but some transitory difficulties, retirement owing to abuse of position, sudden loss through speculation, domestic sorrow and trouble.

With Venus. Strange events, romantic and peculiar marriage entailing separation for Government or political reasons.

With Mars. Difficulties through occult matters, bad for gain.

With Jupiter. Litigation, material and social success, difficulties in marriage, may marry abroad or a foreigner.

With Saturn. Sharp, cunning, dishonest, immoral, cold, unsympathetic, hard-hearted, disgraces an honourable father, hypnotic influence over opposite sex, many intrigues wrecking homes, death through female's revenge.

With Uranus. Occult interest, very unfavourable for women, sensitive, emotional, vacillating, weak mind, easily influenced, led astray in early life, indiscreet actions, trouble through opposite sex, bad for gain, bad for marriage before middle age, accidental death.

With Neptune. Mediumistic, good-looking, youthful appearance, success in occupations connected with amusements or ornament, domestic harmony, many moves and changes, peculiar matrimonial conditions, sudden death.

91. SCALE, NORTH. *β Libræ.* ♏ 18° 15'.

Notes. A pale emerald star situated in the northern scale of the Balance. Its proper name is Zubeneschamali, from Al Zuban al Shamaliyyah, the Northern Claw, a reference to the ancient celestial sphere in which Libra was omitted and Scorpio occupied 60°. It is symbolically called the Full Price.

Influence. According to Ptolemy it is of the nature of Jupiter and Mercury, but later writers have considered it similar to Jupiter and Mars, and Alvidas likens it to Mars in sextile to Jupiter. It gives good fortune, high ambition, beneficence, honour, riches, and permanent happiness.

If rising or culminating. Honour, preferment, good fortune.

With Sun. Great good fortune, high position, transitory difficulties eventually proving beneficial.

With Moon. Active mind, organizing ability, benefits through new and influential friends, valuable gifts, uses friends' names to obtain money but matter is amicably settled, high position, love of respectable women.

With Mercury. Active, alert, favours from influential people, good position, much expenditure, benefits through writings.

With Venus. Social success, help from women, favourable for love affairs and marriage.

With Mars. High ambitions, success through energy, influential position, forceful writer and speaker.

With Jupiter. Philosophical mind, ecclesiastical or legal preferment, able writer or speaker, influential friends.

With Saturn. Cautious, reserved, studious, economical, analytical, good chemist or detective, good judge of human nature, early losses never fully recovered, favourable for gain and domestic matters, sickness to children in infancy.

With Uranus. Economical, great self-control, psychic, material instincts, many difficulties, good for gain but much expenditure, loss through law and enemies, help from influential friends, occasional peculiar domestic disharmony, sudden death often from heart trouble.

With Neptune. Occult writer or speaker, medical or chemical discoveries, practical, kind, sympathetic, alive to self interests, gain through marriage and business, disharmony with parents, grandparents, or relatives, legacy obtained through litigation, suffers from accidents, death resulting from previous injury.

92. SCALE, SOUTH. *a Librae.* ♏ 13° 58'.

Notes. A double star, pale yellow and light grey, situated in the southern scale of the Balance. Its proper name is Zubenelgenubi, from Al Zuban al Janubiyyah, the Southern Claw. Symbolically called the Insufficient Price.

Influence. According to Ptolemy and the old writers it is of the nature of Saturn and Mars, but later authors substitute Saturn and Venus or Saturn and Mercury, and Alvidas likens it to Mars, Venus and Saturn. It causes malevolence, obstruction, an unforgiving character, violence, disease, lying, crime, disgrace, and danger of poison.

With Sun. Sickness, loss in business and through fire or speculation, disgrace, ruin, disfavour of superiors, suffers through wrongful accusations, sickness to family.

With Moon. Trouble through opposite sex, wrongful accusations, disgrace, ruin, mental anxiety, loss of relatives, many disappointments, much sickness, disease in those parts of the body ruled by the sign.

With Mercury. Crafty, revengeful, treacherous, quick mind, bad health, bad for gain, disgrace, poverty at end of life.

With Venus. Bad for marriage, sudden and secret death, may be poisoned owing to jealousy of one of own sex.

With Mars. Bitter quarrels, entailing bloodshed or death.

With Jupiter. Hypocrisy, deceit, dishonesty, pretended religious zeal for business purposes, danger of imprisonment.

With Saturn. Dishonourable, often escapes justice but finally suffers, jealous, quick-tempered, domestic disharmony, bad for marriage, gain and legacies; miserable death.

With Uranus. Sharp, cunning, dangerous, abnormal mind, thought reader, always injuring others, may commit undiscovered crime, violent passions but great control, secret revenge, latter part of life in asylum or prison, violent death.

With Neptune. Morose, melancholy, isolated, shrewd, cunning, evil use of occult powers and of poisons or drugs, cynical, dangerous, broods over some secret, peculiar death, often suicide

With Fortuna. Loss by thieves, soldiers, servants, gambling, speculation, fire and lawsuits.

93. Scheat. *β Pegasi.* ♓ 28° 15′.
Notes. An irregularly variable deep-yellow star situated on the left leg of Pegasus.

Influence. According to Ptolemy it is of the nature of Mars and Mercury; to Simmonite, of Saturn; to other authors, of Saturn and Mercury; and, to Alvidas, of Neptune in square to Saturn or Mars. It causes extreme misfortune, murder, suicide, and drowning.

With Sun. Bad for success, danger through water and engines, liable to accidents or drowning.

With Moon. Worry, loss and gain of friends through criticism, danger of accidents and by water, bad for gain.

With Mercury. Many accidents and narrow escapes especially by water, many enemies, trouble through writings, bad for health and domestic affairs.

With Venus. Evil environment, suffering through own acts, danger of imprisonment or restraint.

With Mars. Many accidents, bad for gain, sickness to native and relatives.

With Jupiter. Many voyages, losses through law, friends and relatives, danger of imprisonment.

With Saturn. Danger of death in infancy, bad for gain and pleasure, domestic trouble, colds and consumption, death by drowning or accident.

With Uranus. Deceitful, vacillating, little concentration, psychic, unreliable, bad for gain, involved in difficulties due to own acts, many accidents, death through drowning or by water especially if in 1st, 6th, 8th or 10th houses.

With Neptune. Prominent in inventive, occult or psychic matters, persecuted, peculiar domestic conditions, many accidents, danger of drowning.

With a malefic and Moon with Sirius, death by fiery cutting weapons or from beasts. If the Moon be with Wega, violent death.

94. SEGINUS. γ *Boötis.* ♎ 16° 32′.

Notes. A small star situated on the left shoulder of Boötes.

Influence. Of the nature of Mercury and Saturn. It gives a subtle mind, shamelessness and loss through friends and companies.

With Moon. Preferment by indirect means followed by disgrace and ruin.

95. SHARATAN. β *Arietis.* ♉ 2° 51′.

Notes. A pearly white star situated on the horn of the Ram, and commonly called the Ram's North Horn. From Al Sharatain, the Two Signs.

Influence. Of the nature of Mars and Saturn. It causes bodily injuries, unscrupulous defeat, destruction by fire, war or earthquake.

96. SINISTRA. *ν Ophiuchi.* ♐ 28° 38′.

Notes. A small star situated in the left hand of Ophiuchus.

Influence. Of the nature of Saturn and Venus. It gives an immoral, mean and slovenly nature.

With Moon. Lustful, wanton, infamous, scandalous, addicted to sorcery and poisoning.

97. SIRIUS. *α Canis Majoris.* ♋ 12° 59′.

Notes. A binary star; brilliant white and yellow, situated in the mouth of the Greater Dog. From Seirios, Sparkling or Scorching, or according to some authors from the Egyptian god Osiris. Among these people it was also Thoth and Sothis, and formed the basis of the Sothic period of chronology. The Chinese knew it as Tseen Lang, the Heavenly Wolf, and said that when unusually bright it portended attacks from thieves.

Influence. According to Ptolemy it is of the nature of Jupiter and Mars ; and, to Alvidas, of the Moon, Jupiter and Mars. It gives honour, renown, wealth, ardour, faithfulness, devotion, passion and resentment, and makes its natives custodians, curators and guardians. It also gives danger of dog bites, and two examples of this effect will be found under Procyon.

If culminating. High office under Government giving great profit and reputation.

With Sun. Success in business, occupation connected with metals or other martial affairs, domestic harmony. If rising or culminating, kingly preferment.

With Moon. Success in business, influential friends of opposite sex, favourable for the father, good health, beneficial changes in home or business. If a malefic be with Scheat, death by fiery cutting weapons or from beasts. If Saturn be with the Moon, death by wild beasts or soldiers.

With Mercury. Great business success, help through influential people, worries unnecessarily, associated with the Church, physical defect through accident.

With Venus. Ease, comfort and luxury, extravagant, gain by inheritance.

With Mars. Courageous, generous, military preferment, work in connection with metals.

With Jupiter. Business success, journeys, help from relatives, ecclesiastical preferment.

With Saturn. Steady, reserved, diplomatic, just, persevering, high position through friends, favourable for home, gifts and legacies, domestic harmony.

With Uranus. Gain and prominence in Uranian matters, help from influential friends, gain through harmonious marriage, especially if male; sudden death.

With Neptune. Intuitional, occult interests, religious, good organizing ability, success in mercantile pursuits, banks or corporations, many influential friends, favourable for gain and domestic matters, natural death

98. Skat. δ *Aquarii*. ⓧ 7° 45'.

Notes. A small star situated on the right leg of Aquarius. From Al Shi'at, a Wish, or Al Sak, the Shin Bone.

Influence. According to Ptolemy it is of the nature of Saturn and Jupiter; to Simmonite, of Uranus; and, to Alvidas, of Uranus and Venus in sextile to Mercury. It gives good fortune and lasting happiness.

With Sun. Sensitive, emotional, psychic; criticism and persecution through mediumship, but help from friends.

With Moon. New and influential friends, associated with companies, public position, but little prominence, valuable gifts, love of respectable women.

With Mercury. Peculiar events, occult interests, psychic, many friends.

With Venus. Psychic, occult interests, friends among opposite sex, favourable for gain.

With Mars. Energetic, advancement through exertions, mechanical discoveries or ability.

With Jupiter. Philosophical, occult or religious mind, social success, prominent in Freemasonry.

With Saturn. Trouble through opposite sex, many travels and peculiar adventures, sudden ups and downs, early marriage but may desert wife or be deserted or marriage may be bigamous, separated from children, no help from friends, bad for gain and for health in latter part of life, may die in workhouse, hospital or asylum.

With Uranus. Vacillating, weak character, mentally far in advance of his time, writer on theories of life, suffering from violent attachment or marriage in early life, eccentric, greatly criticized, sudden death.

With Neptune. Abnormal mind, changeable, easily discouraged, idealistic, psychic, many alliances, separated from marriage partner and children, accidents, may become insane, death through a fall or by water in middle life.

99. SPICA. α *Virginis.* ♎ 22° 43′.

Notes. A brilliant flushed white binary star in the Wheat Ear of Virgo. Frequently called Arista.

Influence. According to Ptolemy it is of the nature of Venus and Mars; and, to Alvidas, of Venus, Jupiter and Mercury. It gives success, renown, riches, a sweet disposition, love of art and science, unscrupulousness, unfruitfulness and injustice to innocence.

If rising or culminating. Unbounded good fortune, riches, happiness, ecclesiastical preferment, unexpected honour or advancement beyond native's hopes or capacity.

With Sun. Great and lasting preferment, eminent dignity, immense wealth, great happiness to native's parents and children, help from friends among clergy, favourable for public and legal affairs. If culminating, Church and State preferment. If with Venus and Mars also the native is a potent king obeyed by many people, but subject to many infirmities.

With Moon. Gain through inventions, success, wealth and honour from Mercury, Venus or Jupiter people.

With Mercury. Neat, tidy, clever, ingenious, favour of clergy and people in authority, gain through investment, responsible position.

With Venus. Benefits from friends, social success, false friends of own sex.

With Mars. Popular, social success, may have good judgment and quick decision or be violent in dispute, rigid, and nearly or quite a fool.

With Jupiter. Popular, social success, wealth, ecclesiastical honour and preferment.

With Saturn. Apt to be suspicious, sharp or rugged, but does much good, occult interests, good speaker, popular, many friends, gain through legacies but extravagant, good health, favourable for domestic matters.

With Uranus. Mediumistic, popular, business connected with ornaments, gain through marriage, fortunate, sudden natural death.

With Neptune. Well-born, comfortable surroundings, always sufficiently well off, associated with companies, gain through legacies, favourable for domestic matters, somewhat fast and extravagant, does not live to old age.

With Fortuna. Great wealth, voluptuous propensities.

100. SPICULUM. 8 M, 20 M, 21 M *Sagittarii.*
♐ 29° 32′.

Notes. Two clusters and a nebula (20 M) situated on the arrow-head of Sagittarius.

Influence. Of the nature of Mars and the Moon, and specifically mentioned by Ptolemy as productive of blindness.

101. TEJAT. η *Geminorum* ♋ 2° 19'.
Notes. A binary and variable star situated on the left foot of the northern Twin.
Influence. Of the nature of Mercury and Venus. It causes violence, pride, over-confidence and shamelessness.

102. TEREBELLUM. ω *Sagittarii* ♑ 24° 43'.
Notes. The chief star of " the four-sided figure in the tail " of Sagittarius mentioned by Ptolemy.
Influence. Of the nature of Venus and Saturn. It gives a fortune but with regret and disgrace, cunning, a mercenary nature and repulsiveness.

103. UNUKALHAI. a *Serpentis* ♏ 20° 56'.
Notes. A pale yellow star situated on the neck of the Serpent. From Unk al Hayyah, the Neck of the Snake. Sometimes called Cor Serpentis, the Serpent's Heart.
Influence. According to Ptolemy it is of the nature of Saturn and Mars; to Simmonite, of Saturn and Venus; to Pearce, of Saturn, Venus and Mars; and, to Alvidas, of Mars and Saturn in opposition to Venus. It gives immorality, accidents, violence and danger of poison.
With Sun. Many quarrels and disappointments, unfortunate life, seriously affected by death of family or friends.
With Moon. Clever, evil environment, hatred of authority, involved in intrigues and plots, banished, imprisoned or hanged for crime probably by poisoning.
With Mercury. Dishonourable, accused of forgery

or theft of papers, ill-health, narrow escapes, danger of bites from poisonous animals.

With Venus. Enmity, jealousy of own sex, bad for domestic matters, favourable for gain, secret death probably by poison.

With Mars. Violence, quarrels, lying, crime, violent death probably by poison.

With Jupiter. Hypocrisy, deceit, banishment, imprisonment or exile.

With Saturn. Secret insanity, drug taker, secret crime and poisoning often for no reason, shrewd, cunning, intelligent, studious, often physician or nurse, usually unmarried, may commit suicide or be confined in an asylum or prison.

With Uranus. Spasmodic insanity, wealthy and luxurious environment, often fails to obtain inheritance, bad for marriage, may commit crime, sudden death often by suicide.

With Neptune. Shrewd, ingenious, courageous, persistent, intuitive, evil environment, often criminal, trouble through opposite sex, bad for gain and marriage, violent death.

104. VERTEX. 31 M *Andromedæ.* ♈ 26° 43′.

Notes. The Great Nebula situated to the north of Andromeda's head.

Influence. Of the nature of Mars and the Moon. It causes blindness, injuries to the eyes, sickness and a violent death.

105. VINDEMIATRIX. ε *Virginis.* ♎ 8° 50′.

Legend. Vindemiatrix, or as it was originally called, Vindemiator, the Gatherer of Grapes, represents Ampelos, the son of a satyr and a nymph, to whom Bacchus, in token of his fondness, gave a vine planted at the foot of an elm. While gathering grapes Ampelos fell and broke his neck, whereupon Bacchus placed him among the stars as a memorial of his former affection.

Notes. A bright yellow star situated on the right wing of Virgo. Its name is said to have been given because it rises in the morning just before the time of vintage. Wilson, Simmonite and Alvidas all erroneously place this star in the sign Virgo instead of in Libra.

Influence. According to Ptolemy it is of the nature of Saturn and Mercury; to Simmonite, of Saturn and Venus, which is probably a misprint; to Wilson and Pearce, of Saturn, Venus and Mercury, and, to Alvidas, of Mercury and Saturn in evil aspect. It gives falsity, disgrace, stealing, wanton folly and often causes its natives to become widows.

With Sun. Worry, depression, unpopular, failure in business, harassed by creditors.

With Moon. Worry, many disappointments, loss through law or writings and theft, bad health, failure in business.

With Mercury. Impulsive, too hasty, loss through writings and business.

With Venus. Trouble through love affairs, loss of friends, danger of scandal.

With Mars. Rash, headstrong, indiscreet, energetic, trouble through law, business and friends.

With Jupiter. Trouble through law or Church, much criticism, many journeys.

With Saturn. Cautious, thoughtful, reserved

materialistic, hypocritical in religion, loss through speculation, success in business, secret difficulty with marriage partner.

With Uranus. Deformity or disease of spine or back about which native is sensitive and seeks seclusion especially if female, danger of heart trouble, bad for marriage, death through an accident.

With Neptune. Active, critical, mind hovers between spiritual and material things, loss through speculation and Mercurial matters, mechanical and inventive ability, temporary domestic separations, death of or separation from a child, death through an accident or Saturnian disease.

106. WASAT. δ *Geminorum.* ♋ 17° 24'.

Notes. A double star, pale white and purple, situated on the right arm of the northern Twin. From Al Wasat, the Middle.

Influence. Of the nature of Saturn. It gives violence, malevolence, destructiveness as a first principle, and is connected with chemicals, poisons and gas.

107. WEGA. α *Lyræ.* ♑ 14° 12'.

Notes. A pale sapphire star situated in the lower part of the Lyre. From Al Waki, the Falling, and known in the Middle Ages as Vultur Cadens, the Falling Grype or Vulture. Often incorrectly spelt Vega.

Influence. According to Ptolemy it is of the nature of Venus and Mercury ; and, to Alvidas, of Saturn in trine to Jupiter from the earthy signs especially Capricorn and Taurus. It gives beneficence, ideality, hopefulness, refinement and changeability, and makes its natives grave, sober, outwardly pretentious and usually lascivious.

With Sun. Critical, abrupt, reserved, unpopular, fleeting honours, influential position, insincere friends. If with Mars also, above the earth, and the Moon be with Procyon, death from the bite of a mad dog.

With Moon. Public disgrace, probably through forgery, loss through writings, some ill-health, success in business, gain through an annuity or pension. If a malefic be with Scheat, violent death.

With Mercury Suspicious, reserved, bitter, thwarted ambitions, double dealing, secret enemies in influential positions, trouble with the mother, loss in business.

With Venus. Hard-hearted, cold, miserly ; ill-health, ugliness or deformity.

With Mars. Scientific interests, unpopular opinions, moral courage, favourable for gain.

With Jupiter. Loss through legal affairs, favourable for gain, danger of imprisonment.

With Saturn. Strong passions, opinionated, original, many Mercurial difficulties, reputation suffers through wrongful accusations, trouble with superiors, domestic difficulties, few, if any, children, latter half of life more favourable, sudden death.

With Uranus. Critical, abrupt, reserved, strong passions, materialistic, many disappointments, domestic sorrow, much gain and loss, many open and secret enemies, accidental or violent death.

With Neptune. Timid, fond of music, occult interests, practical and scientific mind, associated with occult societies, material success, home may be broken up, liable to accidents, natural death in old age especially when Mars is in favourable aspect.

108. YED PRIOR. δ *Ophiuchi.* ♐ 1° 11'.
Notes. A deep yellow star situated on the left hand of Ophiuchus. From Yad, the Hand.
Influence. Of the nature of Saturn and Venus. It causes immorality, shamelessness and revolution.

109. ZANIAH. η *Virginis.* ♎ 3° 43'.
Notes. A variable star situated on the southern wing of Virgo. From Al Zawiah, the Angle or Corner which formed part of the Kennel of the Barking Dogs located here by the Arabs.
Influence. According to Ptolemy it is of the nature of Mercury and Venus ; and, to Alvidas, of Venus and Mercury in sextile. It gives refinement, honour, congeniality, order and a lovable nature.
With Sun. Educational and studious interests, popular, social success, much pleasure, favourable for marriage.
With Moon. Worry, loss through legal and Venusian affairs, trouble through writings, led astray by sympathies.
With Mercury. Musical or artistic ability, gain through writing short stories, popular, social success, many friends especially among opposite sex.
With Venus. Quick in learning, musical and artistic ability, fond of society, many friends, favourable for gain.
With Mars. Active, energetic, loss through lawsuits, trouble through opposite sex.
With Jupiter. Religious and philosophical mind, social success, many friends.

With Saturn. Sober, industrious, many influential elderly friends, gain through old people, grandparents, and marriage.

With Uranus. Studious, psychic, retiring, somewhat unpractical, uneventful life, many friends, social success, favourable for marriage if male but less so if female, gain through marriage and business, natural death.

With Neptune. Kind, sympathetic, somewhat impatient, good at detail work, peculiar love affairs, gain through marriage and partnership, help from influential friends, uneventful life, danger of death at about 10 years of age or natural death in middle life.

110. ZAVIJAVA. *β Virginis.* ♍ 26° 2′.

Notes. A pale yellow star situated below the head of Virgo. From Al Zawiah, the Angle or Corner (see ZANIAH), but according to Bullinger the name means the Gloriously Beautiful. Symbolically called Correct Weighing. This star was used for confirming the Einstein theory during the solar eclipse of 21st September, 1922, which fell close to it.

Influence. Of the nature of Mercury and Mars. It gives beneficence, force of character, strength, combative movements and destructiveness.

111. ZOSMA. *δ Leonis.* ♍ 10° 12′.

Notes. A triple star, pale yellow, blue and violet situated on the Lion's back. From Zosma, a Girdle.

Influence. Of the nature of Saturn and Venus. It causes benefit by disgrace, selfishness, egotism, immorality, meanness, melancholy, unhappiness of mind and fear of poison, and gives an unreasonable, shameless and egotistical nature.

CHAPTER VI

THE FIXED STARS IN MUNDANE ASTROLOGY

VERY little is known as to the effect of the fixed stars in mundane astrology although there is no doubt that their influence is of supreme importance in this branch of the subject. In matters concerning the fate of nations and cities the movement of the planets is too rapid to cause radical changes They do indeed effect the more ephemeral happenings, but for slow, world-wide changes and epoch-making events it is necessary to take note of influences that are correspondingly great, and we are driven to a consideration of the movement of stars as being the only influence known to us that is capable of producing effects of the necessary magnitude. Unfortunately circumstances are against any detailed examination of this nature owing to the immense periods of time involved, and therefore our knowledge is of the smallest, but nevertheless one or two facts are on record and with an increased interest in astrology others will no doubt rapidly come to light. The growth of religions appears to be in some way connected with the passage of the vernal equinox through the zodiac of constellations. Thus its entry into the constellation Taurus is associated with the worship of Baal and the golden calf, and its passage

into Aries with the worship of the ram. Christ-
tianity arose when the vernal equinox was nearing
Pisces and it is significant that the symbol of a fish
was that adopted by the followers of the new religion. A greater amount of detail may be obtained
from a study of the decanate through which the
vernal equinox is passing. The approximate period
during which it remains in one sign is 2160 years,
and it therefore requires about 720 years to pass
through a single decanate, which it does in a retrograde direction. Unfortunately the exact position
of the vernal equinox in the constellations is not
known with any accuracy, but there seems to be no
doubt that the first point of Aries in the zodiac of
signs coincided with that in the constellation zodiac
in about 500 A.D.

In addition to the influence of the moving equinox
itself similar effects are brought about by the same
phenomenon of precession on the longitudes of the
stars, which increase at the rate of a little over 50″
per annum. Pearce pointed out that the Roman
Empire and the Papal power were greatly affected by
the passage of Regulus through the sign Leo by which
Rome is ruled. This star entered Leo in 293 B.C.,
and the power of Rome became fully established.
In 571 A.D. it entered the Sagittarius decanate
corresponding with the great increase in Papal
power ; in 1291 it left that decanate and in the same
year the Holy Land was entirely lost. When
Regulus left the *term* of Jupiter in 1507 the efforts of
Luther were disturbing the power of the Popes, and
when, in 1868, its influence began to be transferred to
Virgo on account of its having passed the 29th degree

of Leo, the French troops left Rome and the temporal power of the Pope was overthrown.

Another method of prognostication by the use of the fixed stars consists in noting the effect of their passage over the Ascendant and luminaries in the horoscopes for the building or foundation of towns, cities and institutions. Thus it is traditional knowledge that ♊ 17° 54′ occupies the Ascendant of the horoscope of the City of London, and it has been pointed out that the plague and fire of London coincided with the passage of the Bull's north horn (EL NATH) over this degree. In *The Horoscope* for May, 1834, Commander Morrison (Zadkiel I) made some interesting observations on the effect of the fixed stars on Liverpool, which are well worth quoting. He wrote as follows :

" In the same manner we have been able to decide that the exact ascendant of Liverpool is 18 degrees 12 minutes of Scorpio. And we find that the *North Scale*, a very benevolent fixed star, first came within the orbs of influence (5 degrees) of Liverpool's ascendant in the year 1558, when the cottons of Manchester were first bartered for wine with the Liverpool merchants. Two years previously King Philip and Queen Mary granted a charter to the town ; in 1570 the first Common Council was held ; in 1596 a vessel arrived with a cargo valued at £1,000 ; in 1626 King Charles I granted a charter to the town, which was made a body corporate and politic, etc., and the trade and importance of the place began to increase. Again, if 18 degrees 12 min. of Scorpio be the ascendant, 8 degrees 55 minutes of Virgo must be the mid-heaven, which has rule over the Magistracy, Corporation etc. ; and a star in the Lion's back, of the nature of Saturn and Venus, bringing *discredit and dishonour*, has been approaching that degree, and is now, in this year 1834, in 8 degrees 55 minutes of Virgo: accordingly, the Corporation, &c., have suffered discredit by the House of Commons having passed a Bill to disfranchise the freemen.

" In 1863, the *South Scale*, a star of an evil nature, comes within the orbs of the ascendant of Liverpool. It will bring serious losses and injuries to the town and its trade for about a few years before ; but it is not a very powerful star. In 1916, the *North Scale* reaches 18 deg. 12 min. of Scorpio, and will produce wonderful improvements in Liverpool. Some freak of nature brings great improvement to the entrance of the port, and, altogether, Liverpool will *flourish greatly* about the early part of the 20th century.

" In the year 1721, the star *Rigel* came to within orbs of London's ascendant, and that nefarious scheme the South Sea Bubble almost ruined its citizens. In 2077 that star will cross the degree of London's ascendant ; about which period we believe that some ill-advised laws, and many misfortunes, will bring ruin and disgrace on the trade of London. The commerce of that port will dwindle away, and London become very unfortunate. Again, about 389 years hence, the very violent and evil martial star *Aldebaran* enters within orbs of London's ascendant, and then very many evils, including *fire, war* and *bloodshed*, will overthrow the importance of London entirely. *It will fall from its metropolitan rank*, and become far below the town of Liverpool in consequence. Just 68 years afterwards, the very powerful *regal* star The LION'S HEART enters within orbs of the mid-heaven of Liverpool ; which will then become (about the year 2291) THE ROYAL AND METROPOLITAN CITY OF ENGLAND, AND THE SEAT OF GOVERNMENT."

Methods such as these are of great interest but are very limited in their application, for our knowledge of the ruling degrees of towns is far from complete. We need a method of more general utility. In the Middle Ages the Kabalists were in the habit of predicting the fate of nations and cities by observing the fixed stars vertically overhead and attempting to form them into words in accordance with a variant of Hebrew called the Celestial Alphabet, the words so formed indicating the fate of the place. This, of course, is pure kabalism, if not psychism, but it is probable that the underlying idea of the passage of a zenith point from one constellation to another may influence a locality. The position of a city upon the terrestrial globe may bear a definite relationship to a position on the celestial globe. It has been suggested that the meridian of Greenwich corresponds to Π 9°, having progressed to that point from φ 0° during the time elapsed since the beginning of the Kali Yuga in 3102 B.C., and that other places correspond in a similar manner to degrees as far removed from ♊ 9° as the place is distant in longitude from Greenwich, Taurus lying to the west and Cancer to the east. If there is any truth in this theory a point near the knee of Perseus and below the hoofs of Camelopardalis with longitude ♊ 9° and declination 51° N 32' would be vertical to London. A study of such points in relation to the history of nations might throw some light upon events.

In addition to these general methods, however, the fixed stars may be utilized in the ordinary mundane horoscopes for ingresses, new moons, conjunctions and eclipses. Eclipses in particular are important and very frequently affect matters ruled by the constellations in the longitude in which they fall, at the same time stimulating the influence of any star in conjunction with them, and it may be remembered that the great war eclipse of 21st August, 1914, fell almost exactly upon Regulus. The easiest method of interpreting such positions is to consider the nature of the star and also to expand its known influence in natal astrology to cover national events. Thus a star causing sickness in a nativity may produce an epidemic, and one conducing to murder may evoke a series of such crimes, just as Regulus in the case mentioned produced a national warlike feeling instead of an individual one. It has also been said that fixed stars falling on the angles and indeed on any cusp in such maps stimulate the influence of the house concerned in accordance with their natures, and probably the constellations situated on the angles or in the houses are also worthy of consideration.

Before leaving the subject of mundane astrology it is necessary to add a few words on Novæ or Temporary Stars. These are generally included by the old authors under the same heading as comets, and the same significations are applied to both. Their effect appears to be exerted through the constellation in which they appear, and also through the zodiacal sign and degree to which their position corresponds. They are said to cause inordinate heat, pestilences, sterility of the earth, wars and changes in kingdoms, winds, earthquakes and floods, and are assigned to the planets according to their colours. Those of the nature of Saturn cause mortality and beheading; of Jupiter, abundance of corn and fruit; of Mars, war, fire, pestilence, drought and famine; of the Sun, plague, sickness, and death of kings; of Venus, drought and trouble to kings and women; of Mercury, death of kings, nobles, literary people and youths, together with wars; and, of the Moon. great mortality among the common people.

The influence of such stars (and comets also) in the various zodiacal signs is as follows:

In Aries. Evil to nobles, war, death of some king or of a great lady, drought, diseases affecting the head, ailments among sheep, dethronement of a king and rise of common people. If in the eastern part of the heavens when discovered it will operate sooner and cause wide-spread enmity; but if in the western it will be slower causing trouble to kings, and rain, floods and snow in winter.

In Taurus. Harm to cattle, great winds, destruction of fruit and corn, death of some great man, and in winter cold, earthquake and pestilences. If in the east danger of war and sickness, if in the west much rain.

In Gemini. Wars, incest, immorality, death of young people, abortive births, famine, storms and death of birds. If in the east, trouble to kings, and, if in the west, rain and floods.

In Cancer. Destruction of crops and fruit by caterpillars and worms, war, death of some great person, rape, robbery, famine and pestilence. If in the east, scarcity of food towards the latter end of the year. If in the west, benefits to the public from their rulers.

In Leo. Destruction by wild beasts and vermin, trouble to the nobility, war towards the end of the year, especially in the east, and ailments affecting the eyes. If in the east, storms and drought; if in the west, sickness and danger of madness to dogs.

In Virgo. Downfall of kings, trouble to merchants, fevers, abortive births. If in the east, war; if in the west, poor crops.

In Libra. Robberies, poverty, death of great people, plots and treachery, high winds, drought, earthquakes, scarcity of food. If in the east, trouble to countries under Libra and dearness of horses and mules; if in the west, the contrary, but trouble with servants.

In Scorpio. War, rebellion, death of some great man, drought, scarcity of crops, danger in childbirth. If in the east, drought and trouble through beasts; if in the west, locusts.

In Sagittarius. Trouble to nobility and lawyers, danger of war. If in the east, death of kings, robbery and scarcity of food. If in the west, abortive births.

In Capricorn. War, immorality, poisoning, death of kings, religious persecution, hail, snow, cold winter, famine and pestilence. If in the east, overthrow of governments, snow, much rain, damage to crops ; if in the west, abundance of grass and water.

In Aquarius. War, death of an eminent eastern man or woman, epidemics, pestilence, storms. If in the east, abundance of grass ; if in the west, rumours of war.

In Pisces. War amongst kindred, religious disputes, civil war, destruction of fishes and danger at sea. If in the east, universal enmity ; if in the west, anxieties and deaths amongst men in the western or north-western countries, continuing for three years ; floods and death of birds and fishes.

In general the effects begin to appear at a much earlier date if the star is first seen in the east than they do when it appears in the west. Those places in which they are visible and those ruled by the sign in which they appear will feel the chief effect, which is most manifest when the Sun or a planet transits the place of their first appearance or the Sun comes to the conjunction of the planet whose nature they resemble.

It is, I think, clear from the foregoing remarks that we have as yet touched only the fringe of the nature of stellar influence in mundane astrology, and until more is learnt our mundane predictions will remain in much the same incomplete and inadequate state as they are at present.

CHAPTER VII

STARS AND CONSTELLATIONS IN MEDIÆVAL MAGIC

THE magical ceremonies of all ages have been built upon an astrological foundation, and a knowledge of astrology was essential to the invocator and maker of talismans who had to perform his ceremonies under appropriate planetary configurations in order to obtain the desired results. Most of the magical ceremonies that have survived in any detail are mediæval, and Hebrew in origin, having descended to us through the works of Cornelius Agrippa and others. These processes are largely talismanic in nature and consist in the construction of talismans under the influence of the seven planets known to the ancients. The fixed stars, lunar mansions, and constellations, however, were not ignored by the mediæval magician, and, though their use was not by any means common, some account of the talismans and amulets consecrated to them has come down to us, and it is with these that I am at present concerned.

For the benefit of any would-be dabbler in magic who should chance to read the following remarks I may add that I have never attempted to put any of the rules into practice, and include them here only for the sake of completeness and not through any assurance of their efficacy.

In constructing a talisman it was usual to engrave

the symbols and images upon some of the metal or stone ruled by the planet or star, and at the same time to add a text from the Hèbrew scriptures that was appropriate to the result desired. Should neither metal nor stone be available however, virgin parchment might be substituted. This process had to be done under the proper astrological conditions, and in the case of a planetary talisman it was essential for the planet concerned to be strong by sign, angular or elevated, and well aspected, especially by the Moon. Then the finished talisman was suffumigated and worn round the neck in a silk covering. In the case of the fixed stars the process was the same. The stars, or rather those used in magical ceremonies, were given magical seals, all of which will be found reproduced on p. 233, and these seals were engraved on the image cut out of stone. The talisman was engraved at a time when the star or constellation was rising or otherwise strong by house position, and when it was well-aspected or contained a well-aspected Moon. It was then worn round the neck if of a personal nature, or secretly conveyed into a house if it was designed to affect the inmate. In the case of the Lunar Mansions, it was customary to draw the image upon parchment or the metal specified, adding the name of the ruling spirit and offering up suitable prayers and invocations.

We may now turn to a consideration of the magical effect, images, seals, and rulership over stones and plants of the fixed stars and constellations. In the case of the latter the images used were those of the constellation figures.

MAGICAL INFLUENCE OF CONSTELLATIONS.

1. ANDROMEDA. Gives love between husband and wife and reconciles adulterers.

2. AQUILA. Gives new honours and preserves the old.

3. ARA. Gives chastity.

4. ARGO NAVIS. Gives security on the waters.

5. CANIS MAJOR. Cures dropsy, resists plague, and preserves from beasts.

6. CASSIOPEIA. Restores weak bodies and strengthens members.

7. CENTAURUS. Gives health and long life.

8. CETUS. Makes one amiable, prudent, happy by sea and land, and helps to recover lost goods.

9. CYGNUS. Frees from palsy and the quartan ague.

10. DRACO. Gives craft, ingenuity, and valour.

11. HERCULES. Gives victory in war.

12. HYDRA. Gives wisdom and riches, and resists poisons.

13. LEPUS. Guards against deceit and madness.

14. LYRA. Preserves phrenetical and mad people.

15. OPHIUCHUS. Drives away poisons and cures venomous bites.

16. ORION. Gives victory.

17. PEGASUS. Prevails against diseases of horses and preserves horsemen in battle.

18. PERSEUS. Frees from envy and witchcraft and preserves from lightning and tempests.

19. URSA MAJOR and URSA MINOR. Give craft, ingenuity and valour.

MAGICAL INFLUENCES OF FIXED STARS.

1. ALDEBARAN.

Rules. Carbuncle, ruby, milky thistle, and " matry-silva."

Image. The likeness of God, or of a flying man. It is said to give riches and honour.

2. ALGOL.

Rules. Diamond, black hellebore, mugwort.

Image. A human head cut off at the neck. It gives success to petitions, makes the wearer bold and magnanimous, preserves the body, protects against witchcraft, and turns evil and spells back upon those who work them.

3. ALGORAB.

Rules. Stones of the colour of black onyx, burr, quadraginus, henbane, comfrey, and the tongue of a frog.

Image. A raven, snake or negro dressed in black. It makes the wearer angry, bold, courageous and a backbiter, gives bad dreams, the power of summoning or driving away evil spirits and protection from winds and the malice of men and devils.

4. ALPHECCA.

Rules. Topaz, rosemary, trefoil and ivy.

ALDEBARAN   ALGOL   ALGORAB

ALPHECCA   ANTARES   ARCTURUS

CAPELLA   DENEB ALGEDI   PLEIADES

POLARIS   PROCYON   REGULUS

SIRIUS   SPICA   WEGA

THE MAGICAL SEALS OF THE FIXED STARS.

Image. A hen or crowned man. It gives chastity and the love and goodwill of men.

5. ANTARES.
Rules. Sardonyx, amethyst, long aristolochy and saffron.
Image. A man armed with a coat of mail, or a scorpion. It gives understanding and memory, help against evil spirits, and the power of driving them away and binding them.

6. ARCTURUS.
Rules. Jasper and plantain.
Image. A horse, wolf, or man dancing. It cures fevers, retains the blood and acts as an astringent.

7. CAPELLA.
Rules. Sapphire, horehound, mint, mugwort and mandrake.
Image. A man playing musical instruments. It makes the wearer honoured and exalted before nobility and cures the toothache.

8. DENEB ALGEDI.
Rules. Chalcedony, marjoram, mugwort, nip and mandrake root.
Image. A hart, goat, or angry man. It gives prosperity and increased wrath.

9. PLEIADES.
Rules. Crystal and the stone Diodocus, the herb Diacedon, frankincense, fennel and quicksilver.
Image. A little virgin or a lamp. It strengthens the eyesight, assembles spirits, raises winds and reveals secret and hidden things.

10. POLARIS.
Rules. Lodestone, succory, mugwort, periwinkle flowers, and the tooth of a wolf.
Image. A pensive man, a bull, or a calf. It protects against spells and renders the wearer secure in travel.

11. PROCYON.
Rules. The stone Achates, flowers of marigold, pennyroyal.
Image. A cock, or three little maids. It gives the favour of gods, spirits and men, power against witchcraft, and preserves the health.

12. REGULUS.
Rules. Granite, sallendine, mugwort and mastic.
Image. A lion, cat, or an honourable person seated in a chair. It makes the wearer temperate, gives favour and appeases wrath.

13. SIRIUS.
Rules. Beryl, savine, mugwort, dragonwort and the tongue of a snake.
Image. A hound or a little virgin. It gives honour, the goodwill and favour of men and the airy spirits, and the power to pacify nobles and others.

14. SPICA.
Rules. Emerald, sage, trefoil, periwinkle, mugwort and mandrake.
Image. A bird, or a man laden with merchandise. It gives riches, overcomes contentions, and removes scarcity and mischief.

15. WEGA.
Rules. Chrysolite, succory, and fumitary.

Image. A vulture, hen or traveller. It makes the wearer magnanimous and proud, and gives power over beasts and devils.

MAGICAL INFLUENCE OF ARABIC LUNAR MANSIONS.

The following numerical order of the mansions corresponds to that given in Chapter III, the 1st mansion being taken to be Al Thurayya.

1. *For general good fortune and happiness.* In a square table on a silver ring the image of a woman, well clothed, sitting on a chair, her right hand being lifted to her head. Sealed and perfumed with musk, camphor and calamus aromaticus. Ruling spirit, *Anixiel.*

2. *For revenge, separation, enmity and ill-will.* The image of a soldier sitting on a horse, and holding a serpent in his right hand. Sealed in red wax and perfumed with red myrrh and storax. Ruling spirit, *Azariel.*

3. *For royal and official favour and good entertainment.* The head of a man, sealed in silver and perfumed with red sanders. Ruling spirit, *Gabriel.*

4. *To procure love between two people.* Two images embracing one another and sealed in white wax, and perfumed with lignum aloes and amber. Ruling spirit, *Dirachiel.*

5. *To obtain every good thing.* A man well clothed holding up his hands in prayer, sealed in silver and perfumed with good odours. Ruling spirit, *Scheliel.*

6. *For victory in war.* An eagle with the face of a man, sealed in tin and perfumed with brimstone. Ruling spirit, *Amnediel.*

7. *To cause infirmities.* A mutilated man covering his eyes with his hands, sealed in lead and perfumed with pine resin. Ruling spirit, *Barbiel.*

8. *To facilitate child-bearing and to cure illness.* A seal of gold bearing the head of a lion and perfumed with amber. Ruling spirit, *Ardefiel.*

9. *For fear, reverence and worship.* A gold seal bearing the image of a man riding on a lion, his left hand holding its ear, and his right a bracelet of gold. Perfumed with good odours and saffron. Ruling spirit, *Neciel.*

10. *For the separation of lovers.* A seal of black lead bearing the image of a dragon fighting with a man and perfumed with lion's hair and asafœtida. Ruling spirit, *Abdizuel.*

11. *For the agreement of married people.* The images of a man in red wax and a woman in white embracing one another and perfumed with lignum aloes and amber. Ruling spirit, *Jazeriel*

12 *For separation and divorce.* A seal of red copper bearing the image of a dog biting its tail and perfumed with the hair of a black dog and a black cat. Ruling spirit, *Ergediel.*

13. *For friendship and goodwill.* A man sitting and writing letters, perfumed with frankincense and nutmegs. Ruling spirit, *Atliel.*

14. *For gaining merchandise.* A silver seal bearing the image of a man sitting on a chair holding a balance in his hand and perfumed with pleasant spices. Ruling spirit, *Azeruel.*

15. *Against thieves and robbers.* An iron seal bearing the image of an ape and perfumed with the hair of a ape. Ruling spirit, *Adriel.*

16. *Against fevers and venomous creatures.* A copper seal bearing the image of a snake with its tail above its head and perfumed with hartshorn. Ruling spirit, *Egibiel.*

17. *For facilitating birth.* A copper seal bearing the image of a woman holding her hands before her face, and perfumed with liquid storax. Ruling spirit, *Amutiel.*

18. *For hunting.* A seal of tin bearing the image of a centaur and perfumed with the head of a wolf. Ruling spirit, *Kyriel.*

19. *For the destruction of someone.* The image of a man with a double countenance before and behind, and perfumed with brimstone and jet. This was to be put in a box of brass together with brimstone, jet and the hair of the victim. Ruling spirit, *Bethnael.*

20. *For the security of runaways.* An iron seal bearing the image of a man with wings on his feet and a helmet on his head and perfumed with argent vive. Ruling spirit, *Geliel.*

21. *For destruction and wasting.* An iron seal bearing the image of a cat with a dog's head. This was perfumed with hair taken from a dog's head and buried in the place where harm was intended. Ruling spirit, *Requiel*

22. *For multiplying herds of cattle.* The image of a woman and infant was branded with iron on the horn of a ram, bull, goat or of the kind of cattle it was desired to increase, and this was hung on the

neck of the leader of the flock or burnt into his
horn.   Ruling spirit, *Abrinael.*

23.   *For the preservation of trees and harvest.*   The
image of a man planting, sealed in the wood of a fig
tree, perfumed with its flowers, and hung on the
tree.   Ruling spirit, *Aziel.*

24.   *For love and favour.*   The image of a woman
washing and combing her hair, sealed in white wax
and mastic and perfumed with good odours.   Ruling
spirit, *Tagriel.*

25.   *To destroy fountains, pits, medicinal waters
and baths.*   An image in red earth of a winged man
holding in his hand an empty and perforated vessel.
The image, mixed with asafœtida and liquid storax,
was burnt and buried in the pond or fountain
which it was desired to destroy.   Ruling spirit,
Atheniel.

26.   *For catching fish.*   A copper seal bearing the
image of a fish and perfumed with the skin of a sea-
fish.   This was thrown into the water where a catch
was desired.   Ruling spirit, *Amnixiel.*

27.   *For the destruction of someone.*   In an iron
ring sealed in black wax the image of a black man
in a garment of hair and wearing a girdle, casting a
small lance with his right hand.   Perfumed with
liquid storax.   Ruling spirit, *Geniel.*

28.   *For reconciliation with royalty.*   The image
of a crowned king, sealed in white wax and mastic,
and perfumed with lignum aloes.   Ruling spirit,
Enediel.

CHAPTER VIII

THE FIXED STARS IN ASTRO-METEOROLOGY

No account of the astrological influences ascribed
to the fixed stars would be complete without some
mention of their effect upon the weather. In the
17th century astro-meteorology occupied a prominent
position and received a great deal of attention, but
at the present time it has apparently ceased to interest any but the almanac maker, and its modern
followers mostly practise the slipshod and almost
useless method of noting the daily aspects in the
ephemeris and predicting from those alone.

In the old days it was customary to base the major
weather predictions upon the positions of the planets
in the horoscopes for the entry of the Sun into the
four cardinal signs Aries, Cancer, Libra and Capricorn
together with those for great conjunctions and
eclipses. These general indications were then am-
plified by a study of New Moons, Full Moons,
Quarter Lunations and in some cases daily horoscopes.

It is no part of my present plan to describe the
methods and rules at length, but merely to draw
attention to the fact that in the following account
of stellar influences the positions are understood
to be those occurring at significant epochs, such as

Ingresses and Lunations, and not merely daily transits.

The general type of effect appears to follow the nature of the star. Thus the Sun being with Satur nian stars is said to indicate cold, rain or snow ; with Jupiterian stars, a serene and temperate air ; with Martial stars, thunder-storms ; with Venusian stars, rain, moisture and mist; and, with Mercurial stars, wind. Much importance was attached to the rising and setting of stars, especially in their re-lationship to the Sun, and it is a well-known fact that the ancient Egyptians began their New Year at the time when Sirius rose with the Sun at the Summer Solstice and marked the beginning of the inundations. All the ways in which a star could rise or set with the Sun were carefully classified in very early times and given distinctive names, but only two need concern us here, namely, *Matutine* and *Vespertine*, the former of which is applied to a star that rises and sets before the Sun, and the latter to one that rises and sets after it.

In addition to the individual star influences, the lunar mansion in which a lunation, ingress or con-junction fell was held to affect the weather in ac-cordance with its nature. The meteorological na-ture of each of the Arabic mansions has been handed down to us, and, beginning with Al Thurayya, is as follows : 1, Moist and cold ; more cold. 2, Dry. 3, Temperate. 4, Moist. 5, Cloudy and tempest-uous. 6, Dry. 7, Moist. 8, Temperate and cold 9, Moist. 10, Temperate. 11, Temperate. 12, Moist. 13, Cold and moist. 14, Moist. 15, Dry. 16, Moist.

17, Temperate.   18, Temperate.   19, Moist.   20,
Temperate.   21, Temperate.   22, Dry.   23, Dry.
24, Moist.   25, Temperate.   26, Temperate.   27, Dry.
28, Moist.

We may now turn to the separate star influences,
which, together with those of a few constellations, are
as follows :

ACHERNAR.
With Sun.   Serene and temperate.
With Jupiter.   Serene.

ADHAFERA.
With Mercury.   Moist and windy.
With Jupiter.   Winds.

ALDEBARAN.
With Sun.   Turbid, windy and wet.   If rising
with Sun, wind, rain, thunder and lightning.
With Mars rising or setting.   Turbulent, windy
and often sultry weather.

ALGOL.
With Sun rising.   Snow.
With Saturn.   Cold and moist.

ALPHARD.
With Sun rising.   Cloudy season.

ALPHECCA.
With Mars rising or setting.   Turbulent, windy
and often sultry weather.
With Jupiter and afflicted by Mars.   Wind and
hail, thunder in summer, warmer in winter especially
if Jupiter be stationary.
With Saturn.   Moist and cloudy, sometimes snow
and rain.

ALTAIR.

If rising in evening. Tempests.

With Sun rising. Snow. If matutine setting, great heat and south wind.

With Mercury. Snow or rain.

With Mars. Rain, snow, great cold. If rising or setting, turbulent, windy and often sultry weather.

With Jupiter and afflicted by Mars. Wind and hail, thunder in summer, warmer in winter especially if Jupiter be stationary.

ANTARES.

With Mars rising or setting. Turbulent, windy and often sultry weather.

ARCTURUS.

If there be showers at the matutine rising of Delphinus there will be none at the rising of Arcturus.

If setting. South wind.

With Sun. Vespertine rising, tempests; matutine setting, good weather and showers.

With Mars. Strong winds, rain, thunder and lightning. If rising or setting, turbulent, windy and often sultry weather.

With Jupiter and afflicted by Mars. Wind and hail, thunder in summer, warmer in winter especially if Jupiter be stationary.

With Saturn. Wind and rain.

Rising or setting with Sun, Mercury, Mars, Jupiter or Saturn, winds.

ASELLI.

If the North Asellus be hid when the air is serene and clear it betokens great winds from the south :

but the South Asellus being hid betokens northeasterly winds.

With Sun rising. Thunder and lightning, showers, cloudy season.

With Venus. Moist season.

AURIGA.
If rising. Rain.

CASTOR.
Rising or setting with Sun, Mercury, Mars, Jupiter or Saturn, winds.

CORONA BOREALIS.
If setting. Tempests.
With Sun rising. Cloudy season.

DELPHINUS.
If at the matutine setting of Delphinus there be showers, there will be none at the rising of Arcturus.

If setting. Wind and snow.
With Sun rising. Winds.
With Mars rising or setting. Turbulent, windy and often sultry weather.
With Jupiter and afflicted by Mars. Wind and hail, thunder in summer, warmer in winter especially if Jupiter be stationary.
With Saturn. Moist and cloudy, sometimes snow and rain.

DENEB ALGEDI.
With Sun rising. Snow.
With Mercury. Cold winds, snow, showers.
With Mars rising. Moist.
With Saturn. Moist and cloudy, sometimes snow and rain.

DENEBOLA.

With Sun rising. Cloudy season.

With Mercury. Sudden change to wind and wet

GRAFFIAS.

With Sun rising. Cloudy season.

With Mars. Cold, rain, snow.

HAMAL.

If rising. Rain and snow.

HYADES.

If rising. Rain.

If setting. Trouble by sea and land especially if afflicted by Mars and Mercury. If matutine setting, rain and south wind.

With Mercury. Winds, showers, thunder and lightning.

With Venus. Moist season.

With Mars. Great heat, clouds and moisture. If rising or setting, turbulent, windy and often sultry weather.

With Saturn. Wind, clouds, rain, thunder.

ORION.

If rising. West wind, turbid air.

With Sun. Turbid, windy and wet. If rising, cloudy season, wind, rain, thunder and lightning.

With Mercury. Winds, showers, thunder and lightning.

With Mars. Great heat. If rising or setting, turbulent, windy and often sultry weather.

With Saturn. Wind and showers.

PLEIADES.

If the Pleiades rise fine they set rainy, and if they rise wet they set fine   (Swahili proverb.)

If rising. West wind.

Vespertine setting. South wind terminating in the west.

With Sun. Wind and rain. If rising, east wind If setting, north-north-east wind.

With Mercury. Wind and rain.

With Venus. Moist season.

With Mars. Cloudy season.

With Saturn. Troubled air, clouds, rain, snow.

PRÆSÆPE.

If Præsæpe does not appear when the air is serene and clear it betokens foul, cold and winterly weather.

With Sun rising. Thunder, lightning, showers, cloudy season.

With Saturn. Wind, clouds, rain, thunder.

PROCYON.

With Mercury. Winds, showers, thunder and lightning.

With Mars. Great heat. If rising or setting, turbulent, windy and often sultry weather.

REGULUS.

Matutine rising. North-north-east wind.

If setting. North wind and sometimes rain.

With Sun. Thunder and lightning. If setting, west wind.

With Mercury. Winds, showers, thunder and lightning.

With Mars. Great heat. If rising or setting, turbulent, windy and often sultry weather.

With Jupiter rising. Fair weather in winter, mitigates cold, increases heat in summer

With Saturn.   Thunder, rain, changeable weather.

SIRIUS.

If rising in evening, tempests.   Matutine rising, produces heat, troubles the seas and changes all things.

Vespertine setting.   South and north-north-east winds.

With Sun.   Fair and warm, thunder and lightning

With Mercury or Saturn.   Wind, rain, thunder and lightning.

With Mars.   Great heat.   If rising or setting, turbulent, windy and often sultry weather.

SPICA.

With Mercury.   Sudden change to wind and wet.

With Mars rising or setting.   Turbulent, windy and often sultry weather.

With Saturn.   Showers and thunder.

TRIANGULUM.

Rising or setting with Sun, Mercury, Mars, Jupiter or Saturn, winds.

VINDEMIATRIX.

If setting.   North-north-east wind.

WEGA.

With Sun setting.   Cold and moist.

With Mercury.   Sudden change to wind and wet

With Mars rising or setting.   Turbulent, windy and often sultry weather.

With Saturn.   Moist and cloudy, sometimes snow and rain.

APPENDIX

1. To FIND THE OBLIQUITY OF THE ECLIPTIC.

Obliquity $= 23°\ 27'\ 8.26''\ -\ 46.837''$ T $-$ $0.0085''$ $T^2 + 0.0017''$ T^3 where T is the time from 1900 reckoned in centuries, being negative if earlier and positive if later.

Example. *Required the obliquity for* 1923.

Here T is positive and less than unity, being $\frac{23}{100}$ or .23, T^2 will therefore be .0529, and T^3, .012167.

Then— $46.837'' \times (+.23)$ $\quad = \quad -10.77251$
$\quad -0.0085\ \times (+.0529)$ $\quad = \quad -0.00045$
$\quad +0.0017\ \times (+.012167) = \quad +0.00002$

$$-10.77294$$

Then $23°\ 27'\ 8.26'' - 10.77'' = 23°\ 26'\ 57.49''$.

2. To FIND THE VALUE OF PRECESSION

Precession $= 50.248'' + 0.000222''\ t$

where t is the time from 1900 reckoned in years, being negative if earlier and positive if later

Example. *Required the precession for* 1st *Jan.,* 1923.

Here t is positive and equal to 23.0.

Then $0.000222'' \times (+23.0) = +0.005$
Therefore $50.248'' + 0.005 = 50.253''$.

3. To convert Time into Degrees.

Multiply the hours, minutes and seconds of time by 15. The result is the equivalent in degrees, minutes and seconds of space.

Another method is to reduce the hours, minutes and seconds into minutes and seconds, to call the minutes degrees of space and the seconds minutes of time and to divide by 4.

> *Example. The Right Ascension of Pollux in time is 7 h. 40 m. 25.4 s. Required its Right Ascension in degrees.*

7 h. 40 m. 25.4 s. reduced to seconds = 27625.4s.
27625.4 × 15 = 414381″.0 = 115° 6′ 21.0″.
By the alternative method 7 h. 40 m. 25.4 s. = 460 m. 25.4 s.
Then 460° 25.4′ = 460° 25′ 24.0″ and this divided by 4 gives 115° 6′ 21.0″.

4. To convert Degrees into Time.

Divide the degrees, minutes and seconds of space by 15. The result is the equivalent in hours, minutes and seconds of time.

Another method is to call the degrees of space minutes of time, and the minutes of space seconds of time, and multiply by 4. The seconds of space should, however, first be converted into decimals of a minute.

> *Example. The R.A.M.C. when Sirius rises at London is 32° 26′. Required the equivalent Sidereal Time.*

32° 26′ divided by 15 gives 2 h. 9 m. 44 s.
By the alternative method :

	m.	s.
32° 26′ call	32	26
multiply by		4

$$129 \quad 44$$

= 2 h. 9 m. 44s.

5. GIVEN RIGHT ASCENSION AND DECLINATION TO FIND LONGITUDE AND LATITUDE.

Part 1.

Log. *sine* R.A. from ♈ or ♎ (or log. *cosine* R.A. from ♋ or ♑).

+ Log. *cotangent* Declination.

= Log. *tangent* angle A.

Part 2.

If R.A. is less than 180° call it N, and if more than 180° call it S.

(1) R.A. and Dec. same name (i.e. both S or both N)
   A + obliquity of ecliptic (23° 27′) = B.

(2) R.A. and Dec. different names (i.e. one N and the other S), the difference between A and the obliquity of ecliptic (23° 27′) = B.

If B exceeds 90 use the *sine* of its excess in Part 3 and the *cosine* in Part 4. The Latitude will then be of contrary name to the Declination.

Part 3. For Latitude.

   Log. *cosine* A (*arith. comp.*)

+ Log. *cosine* B

+ Log. *sine* Declination

= Log. *sine* Latitude.

Part 4. For Longitude. (See Note.)

   Log. *sine* A (*arith. comp.*)

+ Log. *sine* B.

+ Log. *tangent* R.A. from ♈ or ♎ (or log. *cotangent* R.A. from ♋ or ♑).

= Log. *tangent* Longitude from ♈ or ♎ (or log. *cotangent* Longitude from ♋ or ♑).

NOTE.

1. In all cases where R.A. and Dec. are of the same name, and in those cases in which R.A. and Dec. are of different names but *A is greater than the obliquity*, the Longitude is obtained directly from Part 4.

2. In those cases where the R.A. and Dec. are of different names but *A is less than the obliquity*, the numerical result in degrees and minutes obtained in Part 4 must be applied as follows instead of as there shown :

(*a*) *If R.A. was measured from* ♈ 0° *or* ♎ 0° subtract result from ♈ 0° or ♎ 0° respectively.

(*b*) *If R.A. was measured from* ♋ 0° *or* ♑ 0° subtract result from 90° and add the remainder to ♎ 0° or ♈ 0° respectively.

(The *arithmetical complement* of a log. is the number obtained by subtracting the log. from 10.00000 The quickest way to do this is to write down the numbers necessary to make each figure of the log, add up to 9 working from left to right, and making the last right-hand figure up to 10.   Thus the *arith. comp.* of 9.73492 is 0.26508).

6. To find the Sidereal Time of Culmination of a Star.

The Right Ascension of the star expressed in time is the Sidereal Time of its culmination.

7. To find the Sidereal Time of the True Rising and Setting of a Star.

A star can neither rise nor set if its declination exceeds the co-latitude of the place. The co-latitude of any place is found by subtracting its latitude from 90°. Thus the latitude of London being 51° 32' its co-latitude will be 90°—51° 32' = 38° 28', and no star whose declination N or S is greater than this can either set (if in N dec.) or rise (if in S dec.).

The following method gives true rising and setting, and the apparent or visible rising and setting will differ slightly owing to refraction and also to the fact that we are here concerned with the mean places of the stars irrespective of aberration, etc., but the difference is so trifling as to be negligible.

(1) Log. *tangent* Declination of star
   + Log. *tangent* Latitude of place
   = Log. *sine* Ascensional   Difference.

(2) If Dec. of star is N, 90° + Asc. Diff. = H.
   If Dec. of star is S, 90° − Asc. Diff. = H.
   (Reverse the rule for places in S Latitudes.)

(3) *For rising.*
   R.A. of star − H = R.A.M.C. of rising.
   For setting.
   R.A. of star + H = R.A.M.C. of setting.
   (360° may be added to allow of subtraction or deducted if the sum exceeds that amount.)

Convert the R.A.M.C. thus obtained into Sidereal Time by Formula 4. The resulting Sidereal Time may be looked up in a Table of Houses for the place to find what sign and degree occupy the Ascendant.

Example. Required the Sidereal Times of true rising and setting of Sirius at London.

Latitude of London = 51° 32'. R.A. Sirius = 100° 24'. Dec. Sirius = 16° S 36'.

(1)   Log. *tan.* 16° 36' =   9.47438
     + Log. *tan.* 51° 32" =   10.09991

     = Log. *sine* 22° 2' =   9.57429

(2) H = 90° 0' − 22° 2' = 67° 58'.

(3) R.A.M.C. of rising = 100° 24' − 67° 58' = 32° 26'.

Sidereal Time of rising is therefore 2h. 9m. 44 s.

R.A.M.C. of setting = 100° 24' + 67° 58' = 168° 22'.

Sidereal Time of setting is therefore 11 h. 13 m. 28 s.

Looking up these Sidereal Times in the Tables of Houses for London we find that Sirius rises with 19° ♌ and sets with 25° ♉. A further reference to the Tables will show that when its ecliptic longitude, 13° ♋, is rising the actual body of Sirius is in the 3rd House and does not come to the Ascendant for over three hours.

8. To calculate the Aspects to the Body of a Star.

Owing to latitude aspects to the actual body of a star fall in quite different places from those to its ecliptic longitude, except in the cases of the square and opposition. These places may be found as follows :

(1) *For opposition and square.* These points are 180° and 90° from the star's ecliptic longitude as usual.

(2) *For sextile and trine.*

Log. *cosine* latitude of star (*arith. comp.*)

+ Log. *cosine* 60° (9.69897).

= Log. *cosine* distance to be added to star's longitude to obtain sinister sextile, and subtracted to obtain dexter sextile.

The points opposite to those so obtained are the trines.

(3) *For semisquare and sesquiquadrate.*

Log. *cosine* latitude of star (*arith. comp.*)

+ Log. *cosine* 45° (9.84949)

= Log. *cosine* distance to be added to star's longitude to obtain sinister semisquare, and subtracted to obtain dexter semisquare.

The points opposite to those so obtained are the sesquiquadrates.

(4) *For any other aspect* add the *arith. comp.* of the log. *cosine* of the star's latitude to the log. *cosine* of the number of degrees in the aspect, adding the result to, and subtracting it from, the star's longitude to obtain the places of the aspect. If the aspect is greater than 90° subtract it from 180° and use the remainder. The result will then be the opposition point to the place of the aspect.

Example. Required the aspects to the body of Sirius.

Latitude of Sirius = 39° S 35′. Longitude = ♋ 12° 59′.

(1) The opposition falls in ♑ 12° 59′ and the squares in ♈ 12° 59′ and ♎ 12° 59′.

(2) For sextiles and trines :

Log. *cosine* 39° 35′ (*arith. comp.*) = 0.11312
+ Log. *cosine* 60°   = 9.69897

Log. cosine 49° 33′   = 9.81209

Longitude of Sirius   ♋ 12° 59′
                     +   49° 33′

Sinister sextile   = ♍ 2° 32′

Longitude of Sirius   ♋ 12° 59′
                     −   49° 33′

Dexter sextile   = ♉ 23° 26′

The trines will therefore fall in ♓ 2° 32′ and ♏ 23° 26′.

(3) For semisquares and sesquiquadrates :

Log. *cosine* 39° 35′ (*arith. comp.*) = 0.11312
+ Log. *cosine* 45°   = 9.84949

Log. *cosine* 23° 26′   = 9.96261

Applying this distance to the longitude of Sirius as before we obtain ♊ 19° 33′ and ♌ 6° 25′ as the places of the semisquares, and the opposition points ♐ 19° 33′ and ♒ 6° 25′ as those of the sesquiquadrates.

9. To convert Right Ascension into Longitude
    without Latitude.

    Log. *cosine* obliquity of ecliptic (23° 27′)

    + Log. *cotangent* R.A. from ♈ or ♎ (or log.
      tangent R.A. from ♋ or ♑).

    = Log. *cotangent* long. from ♈ or ♎ (or log.
      tangent long. from ♋ or ♑).

    R.A. of 0° ♈ = 0°; of 0° ♋ = 90°;
    of 0° ♎ = 180°; and of 0° ♑ = 270°.

*Example. Required the longitude corresponding
to the R.A. of Algol.*

R.A. of Algol = 45° 44′.
Log. *cos.* 23° 27′ = 9.96256
Log. *cot.* 45° 44′ = 9.98888

Log. *cot.* 48° 12′ = 9.95144

Therefore the longitude equivalent is ♉ 18° 21′

INDEX

In order to avoid parenthetic notes throughout the text, the following index has been arranged to include a complete series of cross-references by means of which a Star or Constellation may be looked up from any one of its ancient, scientific or popular names.